I Was Just Thinking

essays from the edge of all light

April S Fields

Faithful Publishing
Buford, Georgia

Published by Faithful Publishing
PO Box 345
Buford, Georgia 30515
www.faithfulpublishing.com
888-860-5394

ISBN: 0-9759941-8-2
ISBN13: 978-09759941-8-4

©2006 April S Fields All Rights Reserved. Permission is granted to copy and quote portions of this book providing the context is accompanied with the copyright notice and contact details.

All Scriptures are taken from the 1901 Old American Standard Version. Available from www.starbible.com

Faithful Publishing has made every effort to trace the ownership of all quotes and poems. In the event of a question arising from the use of a quote or poem, we regret any error made and will be pleased to make the necessary corrections in future editions of this book.

Cover photo by April S Fields - "Sunrise at Sunset Beach, NC"
taken from the deck of Dr. & Mrs. Karl Bitter's wonderful beachhouse. Thanks to Key-Key and Richard von Lange for inviting us for a perfect "downtime" weekend!

To my (way older) sister, JoAnn, who introduced me to the love of the written word by reading fairy tales to me every night until she left me to go get herself married.

Love you, a

Table of Contents

Enthusiasm	1	Child's Play	80
Bath House Rules	5	Dad	83
Hair	8	Confession	85
Carpe Diem	11	Swinging	87
Good Enough	13	Writing	89
Estate Sale	15	Magic Carpet Quilt	92
Free Tomatoes	18	Christmas Past	94
Doing	21	Downtime	96
Good Deeds	23	Free Will	99
Little Lies	24	On Turning Fifty	101
The Drawer	26	Impatiens	103
Rain	28	Picture Book Grandmother	105
Row	30	Curiosity	108
Thirty Minutes	33	Delusions	111
Why?	35	Saving Summer	115
Boomertude	37	Gardeners	118
Faith in the ER	40	Simple	120
Flaws	43	Champions	122
On Death	45	Fashion Sense	124
Noise	47	Abortion	127
Souvenirs	51	On the Water	130
The High Road	52	Real	132
Fever	54	Tadpoles	134
Disadvantaged	55	Black Truth	136
Birthdays	57	Ping!	138
Morning	59	Success	140
Princess Ha-Ha	61	Snow Day	142
Time	63	Volunteering	144
What I Need	65	Playhouse	146
Faith is a Verb	67	Safe	149
Aging	70	Sunset Point	151
Kudzu Rules	72	Warm	153
Old Friends	74	Paper	155
The Dish	76	Lids	157
Weeds	78	Last Word	159

Introduction

*H*ere's how it happened. I get my morning coffee and open up my email to find this inquiry:

I haven't seen your column in Free Delivery in quite some time. Why isn't it run in that magazine anymore? Your column was the highlight!

I calmly reread this a few times, shamelessly basking in the compliment. When I am at last able to overcome my fluffed ego, I respond that I too noticed it had been MIA for several months and I had assumed it was an economic decision; more ads, less editorial, yadda yadda. I thank her and suggest that she email the editor.

Several days later, another email reports that she had received a response. Seems they still like my column and would use it, "when space permits." Now I'm exhaling. A lingering doubt had persisted that maybe they had finally tired of my ramblings. Afterall, I knew it could happen.

Then, my "fan" (I always believed there was one out there who was not actually related to me) invites me to speak at the Buford First Methodist Women's Group. I pause to consider this. I have spoken to groups before, but it's been awhile. So, I ask what topic she would like for me to speak on, artfully lobbing the ball back into her court, buying me some time.

A few more emails and finally we set a date and I'm left to ponder on presenting something "inspirational" as promised. Email is so easy. One can get oneself into enormous trouble with a simple click.

The idea for this book has been in my back files for awhile but desperation kicked me into finally sorting through sixteen years worth of columns and culling out the ones that I have either had good feedback on or those that have special meaning to me.

I guess we don't really have to know what spark ignites inspiration, but it's good to know it still can happen, even when you least expect it.

Always, April

When you have come to the edge of all light that you know and are about to drop off into the darkness of the unknown, faith is knowing one of two things will happen: there will be something solid to stand on or you will be taught to fly.

-Patrick Overton

Enthusiasm

My kitchen and I took a day off. When you cannot remember the last day you had discretionary time on your hands, it's time to back away from work and go somewhere, preferably outside, and sit. Unfortunately, when I am in the middle of a project, it is practically impossible for me to turn my brain off so I had no choice but to compromise. I headed for the deck, the sunshine, the fresh air, loaded down with my laptop and a stack of cookbooks, among them my mom's Magic Chef Cooking.

I have very few things left to actually hold in my hand that belonged to my mother but the faded blue clothbound book, pages yellowed and fragile, some loosened from the rotted binding, back long since gone, is the best possible thing that could succinctly represent what I remember most about being my mother's child. I'm certainly glad I have it but it turns out that henceforth it will always represent something more to me.

Ninety percent of the memories I have of my mother take place in the tiny breezeway kitchen of our post WWII suburban frame home. I have vivid recollections of the blue cookbook, propped open on the white tile counter top as she deftly moved back and forth from stove or mixing bowl to recipe, checking and rechecking the ingredients that would eventually become a culinary work of art, like, for example, lemon chiffon pie. There was always a faint fog of flour dust in the air whilst she worked her magic, her fingers wearing dough like gloves. My mother prepared meals for her family with the same earnest whole body involvement as an artist plans and executes a sculpture.

My mother cooked. Of course, being a full time housewife, she also washed and ironed clothes and cleaned house, though I honestly have no solid specific memories of her dusting, vacuuming or scrubbing the toilet. This is possibly because I was up and out of the house as quickly as I could to avoid being tagged for one of these jobs. You cannot remember that which you were not around to witness. This speaks volumes about my lack of housekeeping skills. No early childhood development practice.

I could not recall how long it had been since I last looked at the cookbook, forty years maybe, but motivated by the mood I was in and my desperate need for mindless downtime, I was questing for ways to do something and yet do nothing simultaneously. I opened it up and started reading. The first thing that caught my attention was the language of the text. In some ways it seemed a stilted translation of foreign language instructions. You know, the kind you might find accompanying products you must put together with directions written by a Taiwanese copywriter who learned English from TV. Beneath one of the handful of photos distributed throughout the book a caption read, "A Brown and Juicy Turkey Necessitates Lots of Accompaniments". Others claimed "French Pastries Wear a Professional Look" and "Hot Muffins For Breakfast Are Enticing". But the best "Lemon Pie is the Acme of Deliciousness" made me laugh out loud. I needed that laugh. It made me relax and pushed my project to the back burner for awhile.

Doing a first leaf through, I skipped to the back and found that every page of the entire last chapter titled "Lorain Oven Canning" had been hand stamped with a big purple "VOID". I dredged up a deeply buried recollection of asking my mother what "void" meant, and with her customary unflappable confidence, her reply that it meant, "don't do it". It was answer enough for me.

My neurons tossed that back and forth for a while. First of all, I pondered on how different the world is today. Imagine picking up a cookbook and finding the last chapter voided. It wouldn't happen, but if it did, we, spoiled consumers that we are, would expect the book to be marked down as a second. We've come a long way from the days when things were not discarded merely because they weren't perfect. Secondly, I considered how much more personal responsibility individuals were expected to practice. Liability had a much less sinister connotation. Instructions voided meant, *don't do it* and that was that. No worries that someone might ignore the warning and then later sue for irreparable damages done. There were still highly defined boundaries of personal ethics.

Enthusiasm

As I turned the pages, loose newspaper clippings emerged, like unearthed scraps of ancient papyrus. There were also pieces of lined notepaper with handwritten recipes scripted in unfamiliar cursive. Others were distinctly my mother's back slanted handwriting. Speedy Taco Bake, Banana Sauce, Lasagna, Apricot Nectar Cake, Prize-Winning Recipe for Pear Preserves. On the reverse side of the page that recorded the New Rice/Broccoli Chicken Casserole, there was a cryptic single column of numbers totaling up to $69.50. Fifteen, nineteen, eleven, ten and fourteen-fifty. What did these represent? Our house payment was $63 so fifteen dollars was a lot of money in 1950. It was probably a list of monthly bills, an important, must-be-paid group of numbers; sums my mother likely anguished over. The faded ink held tight its original purpose but gave up a greater fact: all things of eminent importance eventually dissolve into benign unimportance, don't they?

One clipping seemed out of place. The headline read: File New Appeal for Rosenbergs. It was dated May 27. This sent me to the Net to search the trial of the century to pin point the year. The famous convicted spies, Julius and Ethel Rosenberg were executed in June 1953 so dating the news story put it sometime between 1951 and 1953. I puzzled over why this information was significant enough to earn a spot of honor in my mother's cookbook. Was she particularly interested in this trial, these people? I flipped the brown scrap over and found a recipe for Home-Made Ice Cream. Mystery solved.

Eventually, with tender care, I returned the clippings and loose pages to their final resting place and closed Magic Chef Cooking. Holding it reverently in both hands, imagining that I could be touching lingering traces of my mother's DNA, I shut my eyes and thought about all the years that had passed from the time that the book was an active, vital contribution to family life to its retirement in my possession. A slow rising realization settled in on me. Another mystery materialized and began to resolve itself as I held the aging physical link to my beginnings and the memories of experiences that forged who I have become.

My mother did not teach me how to cook, per se. She never said, "do it this way" or "here, you stir". I learned the mechanics of food preparation while simply watching, filing away for later the "how-to's". What I learned about cooking and life in general while dodging the flying elbows of the woman, who did everything with gusto, was that anything worth doing is worth doing with enthusiasm. Enthusiasm is never half-hearted or lazy. It is the drive that compels one to toss in a few pecans or cayenne pepper when the recipe doesn't call for it, just to see what different taste might happen. It is the inspiration for risking substitutions instead of abandoning a recipe for lack of the ingredient called for. An enthusiastic cook will fearlessly experiment with the chemistry of food for no other reason than to explore and reinvent, to push the envelope in the interest of variety and fresh experience. Enthusiasm is the secret ingredient in problem solving, the foundation for innovation.

Interesting how something, so imperfect, such as an old blue cookbook could make me understand the best recipe for living that I ever learned from my mother:

Anything we do with shear enthusiasm is well on its way to becoming the Acme of Deliciousness.

No pleasure philosophy, no sensuality, no place, nor power, no material success can for a moment give such inner satisfaction as the sense of living for good purposes, for maintenance of integrity, for the preservation of self-approval.

— Minot Simons

Bath House Rules

I redecorated my powder room this year. In keeping with my obsession with the Beach House look, I wanted to do something fun and casual. The first thing that popped into my head while I was standing in the doorway studying the space was—Cabana Bath House. Yeah! That would do it. So, that's what I did.

Several days later, as I was adding the final touches, I fretted that one wall really needed something, I didn't know what, but was sure I didn't want the typical art thing. Experimenting, I tacked up our collection of old post cards from all the beaches and water resorts we have enjoyed over the years. One thing always leads to another and before I knew it I had also put up a collage of family vacation photos. Then I had one last inspired idea. I drew up a list and called it, Bath House Rules, and put it in the center with the photos all around it.

For the past few months, every time I enter this small, cheerful room, I have to smile. It's like having a mini vacation to the beach just to be in there. I never tire of looking at the photos and the post cards, having added a couple of new ones this past summer from Jamaica and Seaside, Florida. But it is the Bath House Rules that has become the focal point. Whenever guests ask to use the powder room, I smile wryly as I point the way. I always know why they take longer than usual. They are reading the rules. They always come out smiling, sometimes, chuckling, even.

Recently, I was reading them again and realized there was something more to the Rules than that which meets the eye. I chewed on it awhile. Gave it time to work in. Finally, I found I could apply every one of the Bath House Rules to a grander scale than just the requirements for the fair and efficient use of a public facility.

This is what I discovered:
Bath House Rules

1. No loitering

To loiter is not only defined as lingering idly and without purpose, it is also defined as wasting time. So here's a good first rule for life - if you can't figure out how to fill whatever time you have been given with good purpose, at least have the courtesy to get out of the way and give others a chance to use what is available. And for Pete's sake stop whining because you are bored.

2. Conserve water - two-minute showers

Well, here's a no-brainer - be a good steward with your resources and you'll have enough to last you until you don't need them anymore but those who come along behind you will have the opportunity to do the same.

3. Footwear recommended

Keep your CSQ (common sense quotient) fine-tuned and you won't ever be needlessly subjected to nasty surprises.

4. Not responsible for articles left behind

By simply holding yourself accountable at all times, though you might experience regret, you'll never suffer the frustration and helplessness of Victim Syndrome.

5. Turn off shower completely

Pull your head out of the fog and pay attention to the details around you. Treasure is often in the little things you let trickle away into the cracks.

6. No paper towels or feminine products in the toilet

This one is subtle but nonetheless significant. Cultivate a healthy curiosity. Ask "why?" once in awhile. If you don't care about the mechanics of life, so long as everything works magically when you flip a switch or turn a handle, you'll be forever dependent on others in one way or another. A little nickel knowledge can come in real handy when you least expect it. You don't have to understand quantum physics to be mindful of how a septic tank works. This skill will apply across the board.

7. Flush

The defining hallmark of a mature emotional intelligence is engaging in the unconscious habit of having consideration for others, especially and particularly those you will likely never meet.

8. Turn off light when leaving

What will your legacy be when you have finished taking advantage of what life has made available to you and you make your final exit? Will it be said of you that you left this world better than you found it?

If nothing else, you would be fortunate, at the very least, to have it said of you that the world is none the worse for wear and tear for the few minutes you spent here.

Actions have consequences...first rule of life. And the second rule is this - you are the only one responsible for your own actions.

-Holly Lisle, Fire In The Mist, 1992

Hair

I hate to be the one to point this out, but someone needs to do it. I'm referring to this whole hairdo thing. Granted, some people, like, oh say, Meg Ryan, for instance, can chop their locks into stringy, uneven, flippy, wispy, waif-like mops that appear to have been the result of a mean junior high sleepover prank, and yet miraculously still look fabulous. Others, like, for example, middle-aged news show personalities, cannot, or more precisely, and to the point, should not. When I see them, beaming at the camera as though they think they are still in their fresh, naive twenties, I just want to invite them to sit down with me and have a little heart to heart chat. But I can't so all that's left for me to do is think to myself, girlfriend, you are so going to hate that you fell head first into the old up-to-date fashion trap vat. One day, you are going to look at photos of your feather-duster-head-do and wonder what in flaming blue blazes were you thinking. I know this because I have photos of my own coiffure train wrecks but at least my excuse is that I was young, and dumb.

You see, photos are so permanent and revealing. They expose, frozen for posterity, on glossy paper, our failings, bad choices and temporary insanity with a glaringly painful epiphinal truth. On the upside, I can almost chart my progress on my road to maturity by the hairstyles in the photographs of my mindless youth. At least, sometimes I can see progress.

I'll skip past the springy tightly-permed Harpo Marx-like do of my childhood, since my mother was actually responsible for that, and begin in my experimental, impressionable teen years with the beehive. This was a hairstyle so unique, it spawned several legendary tales of the urban genre, one of which involved roaches nesting in the ratted, molded, lacquered, unwashed updo. But, because the fashion pendulum always swings in a great wild arc we soon went from the rat's nest to the long straight, middle parted, flower-child, hippy look. I believe the Beetles are credited with ushering us into the long hair years, but Cher was certainly also our hair role model during this period. Since I notice she now prefers pink, beaded, glittery Cleopatra wigs, I'm rather relieved to note she no longer occupies this lofty position of influence.

For a short period of time, and regrettably, during my final year in high school, the square pageboy was the rage. My senior picture is a fine example of this milestone of hairstyle evolution. Indeed, what was I thinking? It looks as though I'm wearing large earmuffs. And not only that but I vividly recall the pain involved in producing this classic coif of hair coaxed into an unnatural shape. Why did I not know that brush rollers leave hundreds of little holes in one's head when one is sleeping on them? I'm lucky my brain did not leak out. Again, I can console myself with the rationale that I had only just begun my journey to adulthood and could not be held accountable as yet for hairstyle choice.

Then, mercifully leaping past a half-dozen unmemorable do's of the following decade, I find myself staring back dumbly, in a snap shot, all grinny with ignorance and annoyingly proud of the wings shooting out of the side of my head. Once again…what could I have been thinking? One thing is for sure, I wasn't considering a day down the road, looking at those flanged Mercurial appendages and wondering if I had made any progress whatsoever toward maturity by my late twenties.

And then, the fashion pendulum determined we would go from straight and flipped back to the all over, layered curly gypsy and "fro". Obviously blinded by the moment, we thought we were not only styling, we were Urban Cowboys and Flash Dancers. This evolved somehow to the short-front, long-back helmet years, ala Carol Brady Bunch.

By now, you should be getting the point. Hair fashion is really a cruel and fickle friend, if a friend at all and I'm not so sure but that trend is concocted by evil designers who actually hate women and love to see us swept away into whatever diabolical style they can convince us we look divine in, which isn't all that difficult a task, might I frankly add. I can visualize a secret society of stylists who meet every five years, like the mysterious "Color Board", an elite group that determines the colors we use to decorate with. Do they gather in some remote all-inclusive seaside resort to debate and create the next absurd hairstyle, applauding and laughing raucously at the joke about to be perpetrated on us?

Perhaps it is only my age showing but I am starting to realize that the choices seem to be getting worse with time, which leads me to believe they hate us even more than they used to. I don't see this as a good sign, overall, because it also tells me women are not getting smarter and more discerning, but rather we are getting more like our younger selves, foolishly willing to be convinced we look great in whatever hairstyle du jour that is chosen for us, so long as some movie star is sporting it. Adding salt to the open wound, we spend enormous sums of money and not a small amount of time adorning ourselves with these ridiculous styles. And like the clueless naked Emperor, we strut and smile for the camera, imagining that we are hip, chic and bad to the bone. Good grief.

Is it possible that the path to maturity really is a circle and not a straight line as we have supposed?

Whatever is in any way beautiful hath its source of beauty in itself, and is complete in itself; praise forms no part of it. So it is none the worse nor the better for being praised.
  —Marcus Aurelius Antoninus (121 AD - 180 AD)

Carpe Diem

I had no choice. I had a traffic court date and the time on my ticket was listed as 08:30. Though I often arise at 5:00 am, I rarely have to dress and leave the house before sun up. I wasn't aggravated, exactly, but I did feel imposed upon, preferring my easier routine of sipping coffee in my robe until 8:00. Nevertheless, responsibility called.

As I turned east onto Hwy 20, from Peachtree Industrial and motoring toward Lawrenceville, I saw it. Leafless hardwoods and spiky pines on the ridge intertwined like black lace backlit with a huge canvas of sky splashed with bold neon pink, gold and mauve. Late December dawn.

At the top of the hill at 20 and PI, I had the perfect advantage point. Driving straight into it, I could watch it evolve without turning my head, or taking my eyes off the mounting morning traffic. Though it only lasted all of about ten minutes, it was a magnificent, breathtaking show and I would have missed it, if I hadn't have gotten that ticket back in mid November. Funny how things work out when you look for the positive side.

So what? You might ask. The inconvenience and the $45 fine wasn't worth it; it was just sunrise. I would disagree. True, it was only another dawn, not unlike many I have seen before, but this one was important to me because it was a wake up call, reminding me that I hadn't bothered to look up in many, many months. And while I am grateful to be able to work at home and not have the morning commute that so many others are forced to endure, I miss the big sky dawns because of the thick stand of tall trees near our house. Dawns occur, of course, but I don't often witness them. In a sense, they happen without me. This disturbs me.

This also left me wondering what else passes me by, every single day. What opportunities do I ignore? What doors do I fail to open? What gifts do I keep under wraps and unshared? What do I waste? And most importantly, will I be held accountable for these lost moments?

Every dawning, both the bold ones and the gray, unfolds with great promise like a perfect rose. There is so much that can be accomplished during the light hours. Like a gift given but squandered, we think it doesn't matter because another, just like it, will arrive as the earth completes a 360 degree revolution, in a short twenty-four hours. But are we foolish to assume the days are like pennies, not worth much and something of a nuisance, tossing them aside, unused? How can we be so cavalier? So impudent? So arrogant? So busy being busy?

We are born to die, the poet said, and so we are, but before we do, we have something of an assignment to spend the days given to us with enthusiasm and appreciation; to open our eyes and minds to the possibilities of what we could do with the precious minutes granted to us. And when we are done, will it be said of us that we gave it our best? Did we even try? How often did we pause at the wonders and perfect art of a spectacular dawn and consider what our significance might be, in the day just ahead?

Did we seize that brand new day and do justice to its glorious beginning?

Seize the day, put no trust in the morrow!
[Carpe diem, quam minimum credula postero.]
　　　　　　　-Horace (65 BC - 8 BC), Odes

Good Enough

The water was the thing. We wanted a view. The house was less important, although we did require certain amenities like, for example, indoor plumbing. When we found this raggedy little place our eyes and hearts were glazed over by what was described in the realtor's terms as, "a million dollar view". Our five year plan to move to the lake quickly became a three month plan. The revamping of the house then became the five year plan.

That was nearly three years ago and I have never regretted it, though whipping this house into shape has truly been a challenge. Between the two of us, Ron and I are pretty handy. We have carved and mushed and pushed and pulled, tweaking a forlorn and shabby shell with not enough closet space into a home that suits us and our lifestyle quite nicely. The view was certainly motivational. Touching the best of all worlds, we have the woods, the water and on a clear day, the mountains on the horizon. We back up to the west so our sunsets can literally take your breath away at times. I'm not bragging, I'm expressing gratitude here and setting up the scene for a recent personal revelation.

Out of the blue, one Saturday morning, Ron announced he was feeling rather lucky and intended to buy a lotto ticket. He didn't know what the jackpot was but he was fairly sure it belonged to him. I wasn't worried, in the least…at first. During the day his confidence began to chew away at mine and when he declared that with our winnings we would find a "better" piece of property and build the house of our dreams, I humored him with casual agreement, but inside I was hearing a small warning bell.

Sitting alone at my desk in my basement office, I tried to imagine myself in a brand new house. New walls, new, unscarred woodwork, new knobs and hinges and cabinets and floors and ceilings. A cold chill of despair washed down my back. It's not that I am emotionally attached to this place, this building of wood and concrete. I have stronger priorities than that. I was taught by hard working parents to appreciate what I have and take care of it, but not to cling to it. This is a temporal world. Things are not what make our lives worthwhile. So, I had to look a bit deeper to route out what was really bothering me.

Perfection. I can't reach it. In fact, I can't bare it. It is too demanding, too, restricting and too...perfect. I am self-made and so completely imperfect I couldn't possibly exist comfortably in a pristine environment. I'd be like a broken-tailed alley cat in a best-of-best championship show.

As I was raising my family and discretionary money was nonexistent, I made everything by hand. Just because I couldn't buy something didn't mean I couldn't have a close second. Now that the kids are out, and suddenly I have a few extra dollars in my pocket, I find that the real reason I prefer to "do-it-myself" is the personal satisfaction and the individuality creating it expresses. I am proud to say the imperfections in all of my projects have become my hallmark. It comes down to this, for me, good enough is good enough. I am reminded of an old prayer that, paraphrased, says, "Dear Lord, give me just enough ambition to want to improve and enough wisdom to know when to stop and appreciate it."

By the way, Ron didn't win the lottery. He didn't seem too disappointed. I cooed with sympathy, "That's a shame, Dear."

But inside I was smiling and saying, "Thank you, Lord."

Have no fear of perfection – you'll never reach it.
  –Salvador Dali (1904 - 1989)

Estate Sale

*I*t was clean sheets day. I opened the linen closet and discovered my blankets, extra pillows and some sheets strewn about the floor. It was a linen wreck. I smiled. Not a normal reaction, you say, stumbling upon such a mess? Everything is relative. I'll show you.

I don't know what made me stop. The sign was small and handwritten. It said, ESTATE SALE TODAY. I don't usually do garage sales. Perhaps it is because I already have more than enough junk in my own garage, why do I need someone else's? But I was compelled to follow the little signs to a well-groomed older neighborhood, graciously lined with mature trees, and pulled up in front of a pristine brick ranch. Obviously once well-loved and well-lived in, it suffered quietly, enduring the indignities of being invaded by the footfalls of prying strangers.

More little signs directed me to enter through the back gate. I noted the landscaping. It takes years to build gardens and to have lush lilac bushes, camellias and thick mondo grass lining the beds and walkways. Years of tending and caring were evident at every turn. Once inside the gate I found lattice trellises engulfed in ever-blooming roses. Someone must have really loved this place, I thought.

I entered the back door and became just one more intruder into a space that was obviously once a busy private home but was now a market place exposed to the buying public. In the kitchen the drawers and cabinets were pulled opened for full viewing. Plates, cups, bowls, pots, pans, silverware, good, still usable things but sadly no longer needed by the owner. On the wall next to the sink, there was a rack full of collectable state demitasse spoons, mementoes of forgotten vacations probably spanning decades. On the window ledge a drooping potted plant, desperate for water, sat next to a ceramic mug that proclaimed that the user was the Best Dad In the World. Down the hall and in the den, framed happy faces on the walls

I Was Just Thinking

beamed back with convincing smiles, old and young, successfully masking average family life, the good, the bad and the ugly. They contributed to the uneasy feeling that ghosts were watching every move I made.

I wandered through the rooms, one at a time, cognizant that the furniture was once carefully chosen and the drapes special ordered to match the carpet. Looking around at the material goods that remained like silent testimonies to the people who had until sometime recently lived and loved there, I was struck by the enigma of it all. It was all worth something once, all those things, but what was painfully evident was that the worth of it was only relative to what I call the Human Factor.

Granted there are wonderful things that exist well past the original owner. Museums and monuments attest to this. Designated value is often greater for a work of art when the artist and successive owners are long dead. But ordinary things, the stuff of our daily lives, the stuff we work so hard to accumulate, and use everyday, lose their intrinsic significance the minute we can no longer use them. They have no real value except as interpreted by human need of them.

So, one has to wonder why we attach so much importance to our stuff? We fret over stains and marks and dings and tears. We fuss at our kids for scratches and the wear and tear of daily living. We make big deals over the things that have no true worth in and of themselves. And yet we collect, save and protect them, spending incalculable sums insuring them against damage and theft. We even identify ourselves with and by our things.

The last space I examined before I left the estate sale was the linen closet. Neatly stacked, perfectly matched sheet sets and carefully folded blankets sat waiting patiently for someone to use them. I could imagine the clean sheet days in this house. Freshly laundered linens stretched onto beds by the loving hands of the one who washed and dried and wrestled with the folding of them. But without a doubt it was the love in the using them that mattered, not the clean sheets themselves.

The day I opened my own linen closet and saw that my granddaughters, Olivia, Tori and Carly had been playing in there, I smiled because I remembered the linens waiting uselessly in the house that no longer mattered. I knew instantly what did matter, though, was the love I share with my granddaughters, not the chaos they made out of my linen closet. I know what you are thinking, children need to learn how to respect stuff and clean up after themselves. Well, my answer to that is that children also need an oasis from the riggers of learning. Sometimes they need to feel comfortable and not have to look over their shoulders waiting for more instructions on how to behave and how to be.

Messes can be cleaned up. One day, my linen closet doors might be flung open for viewing, everything, efficiently folded, waiting to be used, bought or thrown away. Who will remember my sheets or how tidy my linen closet was? However, I would bet dollars to donuts that the girls will forever remember playing in my linens and not getting yelled at for it. That's the Human Factor thingy again. What I learned at the estate sale is that which is truly priceless is rarely tangible.

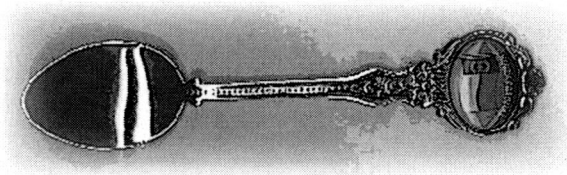

That man is a success who has lived well, laughed often and loved much; who has gained the respect of intelligent men and the love of children; who has filled his niche and accomplished his task; who leaves the world a better place than he found it, whether by an improved poppy, a perfect poem or a rescued soul; who never lacked appreciation of earth's beauty or failed to express it; who looked for the best in others and gave the best he had.

—Robert Louis Stevenson

Free Tomatoes

The packet of seeds came as a bonus to something else I bought in May. In early June I found it in The Drawer where I had tossed it. At that moment I was all caught up in the planting and gardening thing so I put the tomato seeds in a pot and covered them with potting soil. They won't sprout, I thought. But they did. A week later tiny green leaves had pushed their way up to the light of day. Ten days later, to my delighted surprise, I had to make a decision about what to do with the seedlings that seemed to have a focused mission in life. I dug out the seed packet and reread the instructions. Then I went and bought five large planters and three bags of nutritious potting soil and transplanted five happy tomato plants into each planter. I watered them and thought, hmmm, maybe I'll have some homegrown tomatoes after all. The hot, dry summer began to unfold.

By the end of July I had twenty-five robust plants covered with yellow blooms and tiny green marbles that promised to become tasty ripe red fruits to put on sandwiches and in salads. I checked them everyday for progress. Sometimes I gave them a treat with plant food enhanced water. They rewarded me by growing tall and lush. So tall, in fact, I had to go buy stakes to keep them from falling over. Fifteen stakes, to be exact, three for each planter. I could almost taste the juicy tomatoes that would come from the florishing plants in the only sunny spot in my yard, on the deck. How convenient to be able to step out the kitchen door every morning and monitor their daily progress, I mused. I was beginning to think of myself as a true gardener. I envisioned more planters with squash and lettuce for the next summer. My thoughts strayed to vague plans for irrigation. Perhaps I would write a book,one day, about deck gardening.

Soon it was August. Hotter and even dryer. But I have a water barrel on my deck that catches and stores water coming off the roof when it rains. My tomato plants did not languish for lack of water. They grew even taller and greener. Then one morning I noticed several leaves were missing and one of the green marbles was minus a huge chunk out of one side. A closer look revealed definite teeth marks. Oh, bugs, I thought. I'm nothing if not intuitive.

I went to the nursery and bought an all natural bugacide that promised to do the job and sprinkled it all over my precious tomato plants. They looked as though it had snowed. I wondered if I had over-done it. Obviously not, because two days later I found a huge, green, healthy caterpillar munching contentedly on one nearly denuded branch. I gasped and did the first thing that came to mind and went straight to the Internet. I typed in "green caterpillar." I was given about a dozen different websites that offered to inform me about green caterpillars. After reading for an hour, I learned that the official name for these fat hungry insects is Horned Green Caterpillar, affectionately called "mater bugs." They are called this because they live to eat tomato plants. Furthermore they are the pupae stage of a rather interesting insect called a Hummingbird Moth, the life cycle of which evolves around laying eggs on the leaves of and eventually destroying tomato plants. Mater bugs have two natural predators, a small wasp that lays its eggs on the back of the caterpillar which then hatch and eat the caterpillar …. and I. Carefully searching for and removing six, three inch long, tomato plant eating mater bugs, I sent them to mater bug heaven. Thanks to the Net, once again, disaster successfully averted. In late August, my mother in law, Mary, was admiring my well-nurtured tomato plants as I explained what I had learned about big green caterpillars. She blinked and offered that I knew way too much about the subject.

Hot dry August passed into hot dry September.

One morning in mid-September I discovered my first red product of months of watering, monitoring and protecting. It was approximately 2 inches in diameter. I determined it wasn't going to get bigger, so with a mild sense of accomplishment I plucked it. Later I added it to our salad. It was good, albeit somewhat diminutive. Over the next week I harvested several ripened fruits a day, none bigger than two inches, most just over an inch and a half. By the end of September, by exact count, I reaped fifteen small tomatoes. The plants however, are still, at this writing, quite lush and healthy. It's the tomatoes that seem to be missing.

A case of over-nurturing perhaps.

There has to be a lesson in this experiment. On the day I picked the last tiny tomato I did a quick mental calculation of how much it cost to produce. Including the planters, soil, stakes, plant food and insecticide, I concluded that mater cost me in the range of $4.00. I have come to two conclusions:

First of all, I have had to face certain facts about myself, farming is not one of my best things. But that's okay, it is good to know these sort of truths about yourself. It means you are better prepared not to make ill-fated life choices.

Secondly, I conclude that free tomatoes are entirely too expensive.

I would feel more optimistic about a bright future for man if he spent less time proving that he can outwit Nature and more time tasting her sweetness and respecting her seniority.

-E. B. White (1899 - 1985)

Doing

My house guest liked what I had done to my porch, especially the floor. She said she had believed it was real flagstone instead of just paint. She said she wished she could do something like that. I told her she could; all she needed was three or four colors of acrylic concrete paint, some rags, a sponge, kneepads and a weekend. She laughed.

Yeah right, she said, then added that she had purchased some wall transfers from QVC months ago and still couldn't decide where to put them. So, she hasn't put them anywhere. Wish I had a dollar for every time I've heard this complaint. If there had been time I would have told my guest what I know, from first hand experience about this affliction, what it stems from and the road to take to find the cure for it. If she had really wanted to know. Some people would prefer to take refuge behind the problem instead of facing it. Granted, it is easier.

When I had my art and gift shop on Main Street in Buford, I heard this over and over. "I'm just not very creative," I'd hear. I always asked why they felt that way. The excuses ran from, "I can't draw a straight line", to "I can't put things together, I have no vision". A little deeper dig nearly always revealed that the real issue was not creativity, (or lack thereof) but plain old indecision born of lack of confidence and that age-old nemesis of progress, fear of failure. What would others think if it didn't turn out right? How to begin, how to trust the original inspiration, and/or desire to create something in the first place? How to risk falling short?

The simple solution for this all too common problem requires complete abandonment of the what-ifs. What if I mess up the wall/floor/wood? What if it doesn't turn out like I wanted it to? What if it looks like a baboon had been turned loose with it and my friends/family make fun of me?

To the what-ifs I say, so what? What if you don't like it and you have to repaint the wall/floor/wood? So what? What if your skills fall short of your dream or vision? So what? What if, in the end, you spent your time, effort and money for materials and end up with something that has to be thrown away? So what, so what, so what? What if you spend your whole life planning and never doing? How ineffectual is that? What if you never try anything for fear you won't get it perfect the first time? What, I ask, is gained by doing nothing at all?

In my not-so-humble opinion, the core of the issue is singularly about self-image. We can't allow ourselves to experiment and try new things because we can't risk looking inept or inexperienced. No practice allowed. We choose what we try conservatively, not because we are not creative but because it is a safe position. Unfortunately, it is also confining and limiting. The catch-22, of course, is that the learning, the practicing and the screwing up is what takes us to new heights and builds our skill levels and thus our confidence. It is the trust we have in our ability to attempt and succeed at new things that pushes us into higher percentages of success rates. But the building of self-trust takes time, and often many more failures than successes. I am intimately acquainted with this truth believe me. Ask my sister about my first attempts at haircutting. . . on her.

It is a chain really. One thing links to another. First, you do a thing. You might fail, but you do it again and eventually you are doing it more for the sake of doing it, and less for the final results. Good results, however, do encourage more doing, that's a given. But the ultimate reward comes not just from accomplishment but also from one's can-do perseverance as well as from the complete disregard for what others think about it. Every child who ever held up a newly completed work of art and said," I did it myself" knows the unadulterated joy of self-trust. Once you transcend this obstacle you begin to understand the secret of genuine creativity:

Doing is infinitely better than not doing and being is better than doing. But you cannot *be* unless and until you *do*.

Just do it
-Nike®

Good Deeds

"What great deed would you do in life if you knew you could not fail?"

I'm driving along and see this sign. My first reaction is, easy, I'd make sure no one ever went to bed hungry. No Wait! I'd see to it everyone had a home. Nope, that's not quite it either. Okay, I'd eliminate unemployment. How's that? Not bad. Hold on here, let me think about this.

How ridiculous. I'm cruising down the road suddenly obsessed by trying to solve the world's worst problems feeling increasingly frustrated because I can't get a handle on it. I know I can't single-handedly stop hunger, homelessness and the basic human pain that has been around since Cain snuffed Abel, but I really do want to do more than feel smug about what I would do if I could. It's a mid-life need to accomplish something meaningful before I die thingy. But what? I work on it all day. It hovers over me, mocking and teasing me pointing out my considerable shortcomings. By the end of the day I still can't muster up the panacea I had earlier thought would come at the snap of my fingers. I find it's a pitted road from aphorism to reality. You have to do a lot of dodging and weaving.

As the sun is setting, I'm feeling as though I've been given one wish like a silver dollar. It'll only go so far and I desperately don't want to squander it. Why is this so hard? All I want is a clean and real answer. And then it hits me.

What if I reached for goodness on a more realistic plane? What if the best good deed in life was simply the sum total of all the small good deeds anyone performs routinely? If I could live each day with my needs less important than others and offer to share with those who have less than I, then haven't I lived a good deed? This is reality, not platitude.

What is real is half way home to possible.

I spend my wish.

Little Lies

It has been so subtle, a process that has taken decades, we didn't even realize it was happening. It has been happening though, and the results have changed the way we feel about lies and lying. It has come to the point where most of the time, we even expect it, accepting it as the norm instead of challenging it. This revelation hit me like a wrecking ball one morning as Ron was pressing a pair of pants. He said, "wrinkle free, yeah, right!"

Such a little thing, you say? But think about that and all the other little lies we are spoon fed every single day of our lives. Words and combinations of words are what make up our language. If we become desensitized to the meanings of words, we lose, bit by bit our base line. It is this base line that gives us concrete definitions and foundations for our principles. Redefinitions of even the simplest words can alter whole belief systems. For example, thanks to our president we now have a whole new definition for sex, or should I say, lack of sex. The ramifications to this particular evasive language abuse have only begun to emerge.

I'll tell you where I believe it all began. Advertising. It's no secret that lies have been the mainstay of all advertising since the traveling salesmen of colonial days stood and swore the elixir he could provide was the cure all for everything from arthritis to croup. People fell for it then too. We are always eager to believe a cure for what ails us is only a bottle of nasty tasting liquid away. The difference, though, is modern technology and the Information Age. The advent of television was the first big leap to selling huge numbers of lies to huge numbers of people. And the ribbon on the package is slick presentation. I know whereof I speak, in this regard, because I was a contributor to the process when I worked as a commercial photo stylist. I know all the tricks. Let me share.

Let's say, for example, you are looking to buy a new comforter for your bed. You find the one you like and you are most certainly enticed by the great photo on the insert card. There's your comforter, lush and thick, pulled off the bed ever so slightly, the sheets rippling in soft folds over the top. The room is inviting, maybe a breeze gently lifting the gauzy window fabric. You want to just dive in, don't you ? You rush home with your new purchase and rip everything off the bed. You spend an hour trying to make it look as thick as the photo. You try everything you can think of to get the flanges on the shams to stand up all perky - like the photo. You do what you can, but it just isn't like - the photo. Guess why. A stylist spent the better part of two days creating that lovely bedroom scene. And it was just a scene, a set in a studio. Some of the tools she used to make it look like a queen's boudoir were: an iron, steamer, tape, pins, more tape, paint cans to prop up the pillows, and batting on the mattress and under the folds to make the bed look "fluffy". She pulled and tugged and pushed and crawled on the floor, pinning and tapping the bedskirt into perfect alignment. She worked back and forth between the set and the camera looking in the view finder so she wouldn't have to waste time styling anything the camera didn't see. And believe me, there is plenty the camera doesn't see. The result of this labor is a perfect set and a perfect lie. Because the truth is, the comforter can never be, in life, the way it is styled for the photo.

The issue here, though, is not about the lie but rather our complacency and acceptance of the lie. All I am asking is, why is this okay? What damage is being done when we allow this to be okay? What values are eroded? Our attitude about what is not true has been slowly evolving to the point where we don't care what is false anymore. I don't know about you, but I see this as a very bad sign. Historically, society at its peak always holds truth up as its standard.

To let this slide is to allow civilization to sink. Think about it.

Repetition does not transform a lie into a truth.
-Franklin D. Roosevelt (1882 - 1945)

The Drawer

*I*t was a rainy day. But it was a Meema Day so the weather didn't matter so much. Hayes, Olivia and I had things to do. After we baked cookies, Hayes asked timidly, (as if he had ever had a request turned down by me) "Meema, can we make a tent?" What a great idea! They rearranged the living room while I pulled out sheets. Soon one tent grew into a colony and while I finished cleaning the kitchen, the architect and his sister fine tuned the fabric city emerging in my house.

And then Hayes asked, "Meema, can we make a van out of your chairs?" His sweet face all sweaty from heavy labor, hazel eyes sparkling with youthful energy and creativity. It didn't take long for six dining room chairs to assume position, three rows of two. And then Hayes had one more question.

"Meema, we need a key for our van. Do you have an old key or something?" Oh those eyes, looking up at me. Inspired, I knew right where to look. The drawer.

Everyone has one. We all know this. It's the universal, no need to translate, drawer somewhere in the kitchen that has everything in it that can't be put somewhere else because there is no real category for it.

I opened it carefully because it hadn't been cleaned out for a while and things were prone to spring out as if propelled. I removed the top two layers which were primarily coupons pre-1994, flyers from entrepreneurs wanting to clean my gutters and deliver wood, odd photographs, sales receipts, owners manuals for appliances I don't have anymore, and a lengthy newspaper article the importance of which had been long forgotten. I stopped to examine a phone number scribbled on an envelope. Was this important? Should I save this? Would I ever dial this number not knowing who owned it? I decided to save it and continued the dig with the expertise of a seasoned archeologist. With the paper layers removed the hardware layer was revealed. Nuts and bolts, pennies, single earrings

(I know I'll come across the mates someday), allen wrenches that only fit some item, probably sold at a garage sale years ago. Lip balm (that's where that was), a pair of rusty tweezers (oh yeah, like I'd really use those again), Summer Olympic medallions of chocolate. (Hide that, Hayes is watching).

And Hayes was indeed watching.

As I pulled out more bits and pieces, his wonderful hazel eyes widened. And then he said with reverence and awe, "Meema, it's like a magic drawer, isn't it?" I looked again at the growing pile of useless junk but with a new vision - one with a five year old's insight. It was marvelous. Tiny treasures, all with endless potential, though many without definition. Also there were two keys and believe it or not, two key holders, one red and rubbery like gummy worms and one rich looking with the crest of a car maker on a leather fob. The dig was a success. Hayes and Olivia played for two hours in their make believe world, taking turns being driver and passenger of "the van." I took advantage of the moment to clean out the drawer. There was no way I would have been able to get it all back in anyway. I believe this phenomenon is covered by a law of physics.

It was hard. Oh, I didn't have much trouble throwing out the expired coupons and flyers, and petrified cough lozenges, but what about that strange looking screw? What if I needed just that screw to repair something major, like the refrigerator? If I threw it away, you know I'd need it precisely on the day after the garbage had been picked up.

You see, the logic involved here is actually a form of the misguided reasoning of a pack rat. A more objective person would have asked the question, "What appliance isn't working because this screw is in this drawer?" But it doesn't matter, I saved the screw anyway. With all those papers removed, there was now infinite room. Room to toss in more stuff. It won't take long to fill it up again since we are a nation of stuff buyers and I am queen stuff buyer. But that's okay with Hayes and Olivia because the result of this is - Meema has a magic drawer that always produces exactly what they need.

All Olivia has to do is get Hayes to ask.

Rain

Here in North Georgia, after years of drought, cracked earth, parched fields and a lake shoreline strewn with boat docks abandoned in the red dirt banks by the receding water, it is raining again. Not little pitiful drops, either, given up by clouds too weak to spit, but real, saturating, soaking, drenching, air cleansing, all day rain.

From my vantage point on the sofa, laptop securely balanced, I can see a small edge of Lake Lanier. In tiny increments, it is spreading itself from its four-year exile to resume its rightful place at full pool. Up in the cove that hasn't seen water for more than two years, small trees have sprouted, not knowing they have taken up residence where water usually lives. If the rain continues, the small trees soon will find their foundations flooded. How could they have known they had planned their futures in soil that didn't belong to them? The water will surely win out, though. It will, that is, if it keeps raining.

And here's an interesting twist, though the water claims ownership of this gouge in the topography, when the lake is filled, edge to edge, it hasn't always been thus. This land was once a valley between two hills. Before Buford Dam was built, fifty some odd years ago, here, where I sit on my sofa, was part of the hills and vales of a farm. So, if you were inclined to research the abstract, you could say, in all fairness, that the trees were here first. Or, at least, the ancestors of the clueless seedlings, that are about to be swamped, were here first.

Imagine if today's attorneys could represent the trees in a lawsuit against the lake. Ah, but what was I thinking, that's nonsense. They wouldn't sue the lake; they'd go after the Corp of Army engineers for building the dam in the first place. The trees might win, or maybe not, but the lawyers would make a bundle, that's a given.

See what strange thoughts one can entertain on a rainy November Saturday in front of a hissing fire? Earlier I had begun an ambitious list of

I Was Just Thinking

things I ought to do today. Cleaning my office was the first bullet. Then came laundry. My third entry was ORGANIZE PANTRY, but in a flash of sanity, I quickly crossed that one out. In the grasp of summer weekends that lend themselves so well to working outside, boating and swimming, it is delightfully easy to make mental catalogs about THINGS TO DO ON RAINY, WINTER WEEKENDS. The list is long in the summer. But, when the days are warm, bright and long, inside days are only vague, disconnected memories. The list doesn't threaten.

But now, here I dawdle, needing to firm up and accomplish those tasks I had set aside, with such noble intentions, for days such as this, and all I can want to do is sip steaming coffee by an autumn fire, writing and thanking God for His rain. Occasionally, I can look up and watch the progress of the water's edge as it continues stretching closer to the unsuspecting saplings.

List? For the life of me, I cannot remember where I put it. I'm guessing it's in my office, which I'm sure I'll find when I clean, one long August Saturday, when it's too hot to be outside.

So you see, imagination needs moodling – long, inefficient, happy idling, dawdling and puttering.
—Brenda Ueland

Row

Anyone who has been reading this column for the past thirteen years must have picked up on the fact that I love inspirational quotes. I especially love the ones that have layered meanings that compel you to stop and ponder on the wisdom imbedded. I am so in love with quotes that I have several small books strategically sitting out in my home for anyone to flip through and perhaps discover a nugget of truth or enlightenment.

I even have quotes on my kitchen walls, sage words of insight such as, "***Countless number of people have eaten in this kitchen and gone on to lead normal lives***," and "***Sorrow looks back, worry looks around, faith looks up***."

The one over the back door says, "***When there is no wind, row***." This six-word suggestion speaks volumes to me. I chose it because it reminds me to refresh my attitude every time I open the door to walk out into the world. It tells me to remember what the real goal is, in this life. It doesn't mention sitting and blaming the weatherman because there isn't any wind. It doesn't say to sit and whine about rotten luck and the injustice and unequal divisions of wealth that allows for some to crank up their inboard motors and cruise past others stranded in their little motorless dingies. It simply says *row*. This is one of those wonderfully aforementioned layered quotes too, because it also says something else. It says, do whatever it takes to get the job done. Granted this is somewhat obvious, but it opens the door to other less evident considerations as well.

Stripped down to our essence, humans are needy creatures, but our most important requirements are less about material things and far more about the spiritual. However, this commercially underwritten society that we live in has coerced us into thinking we "need" certain creature comforts and we have to have any number of gadgets and gizmos, aspiring to lifestyles that project a convoluted definition of success. We have been brainwashed to look to acquisition therapy to soothe us when life crashes in on us; when the going gets tough, the tough go shopping. Regardless of the reality that material things do not necessarily equal happiness, we continue on hustling to acquire things so that we might be happy.

This gratuitous, illogical drive to be able to be haves instead of have-nots at any cost has led us down a dangerous path to a sorry dead end. The genuine spiritual need to feel content has been seriously overshadowed by the false satisfaction of mindless material gain. Instead of working to achieve personal best, we work to get stuff. This shallow goal setting has pierced a huge hole in our work ethic. It is a classic domino effect. Without the empowerment of the spiritual reason we work, we are left with nothing but the drudgery of labor. There's an old saying, "it isn't work unless you don't want to do it", that aptly applies here. Unfortunately, when all we do is work to cover our material wants, our work soon becomes our master and eventually something we hate. Understandably, when we hate our work we don't give it all we've got and the product of our lack-luster effort is mediocre at best.

We've all seen the results of this. The clerk who doesn't care if you are helped. The mechanic who can't be bothered to wipe off his greasy hand-print from your car. The waste collector who prefers to slam your garbage can lid down in the flowerbed instead of the concrete drive. The technician who changes your watch battery but can't take another thirty seconds to reset the time. The check-out clerk who doesn't smile and ignores you or worse complains to another clerk about his/her employer or job all the while forgetting to deduct your coupons.

The list could be longer, but you get the picture. A materialistic culture will complain that those who do what is considered menial jobs are justified in poor and less than poor performance because they have poor wages. But I offer that ANY job is worth doing well because in the end it isn't the job or the pay that matters, it is the way we feel about our own performance that sets us up for the bitterness or contentment we take home with us at the end of the day. Pride in a job well done is it's own reward. How's that for a quote?

Nevertheless, regardless of the majority of slackers who begrudgingly clock in and squander their daily chances to excel, there are quiet heroes who simply do the job at hand, with good spirit and champion attitudes. They go the extra mile, they think out of the box, they anticipate need

I Was Just Thinking

and ultimately, whether anyone notices or not, they shine. They know who they are and what they are worth. Their souls sparkle and when they cash their below average paychecks, they don't whine.

They row.

> *Noble life demands a noble architecture for noble uses of noble men. Lack of culture means what it has always meant: ignoble civilization and therefore imminent downfall.*
>
> —Frank Lloyd Wright (1869 - 1959)

Thirty Minutes

We were about five miles out of town when Ron suddenly remembered that he had forgotten his computer. As we were turning around and heading back to the hotel, he said, "This is going to add about thirty minutes to our trip home."

I thought about this and replied, "What is thirty minutes? If we knew we only had thirty minutes to live, it would seem like nothing."

"Everything is relative, isn't it?" He said.

This is where the conversation took a morbid turn, as we motored our way backtracking to where we had just been.

"We feel aggravated when we are told we have to wait thirty minutes for a table in a restaurant, or for a store to open, but we'd feel quite differently to being told we only have thirty minutes before the bomb explodes," I added.

"Yeah, the trouble is we never know when our last thirty minutes has already begun."

We gave this weighty concept a reverent moment of silence.

We pulled into the parking garage and Ron dashed out to go retrieve his computer while I granted this topic the opportunity to bloom in my head as I waited.

We've heard it before a zillion times. We know the aphorisms about living life as though this might be our last day, gathering the rosebuds while we may, savoring every moment, but we still allow ourselves to get tangled up in the rat race and the time crunch. We say we could use more time but then we rarely use the time we have judiciously. We fall with impudence into time squandering habits and then occasionally complain there aren't enough hours in the day to accomplish everything we have to do.

Leaving the parking garage I asked Ron what he would do with his last thirty minutes. He smiled and said, "Telling you how much I love you."

I Was Just Thinking

Suddenly everything that had threatened to be out of our control came back into focus, like the sun burning through a thick fog.

Regardless how many times or ways we are warned to stop and smell the roses, we are not likely to ever spend our time wisely. This is a given. Humans are simply not hard-wired to appreciate each moment as though it were our last. We lose our perspective instantly as the crush of duty, work and responsibilities push hard against us. Ultimately, even though we are rarely given the opportunity to choose how we would spend our last moments on earth, if we understand that, from beginning to end, no matter how busy we are, loving someone else is the best we can do with the time we have been allotted. Everything else is just busy work.

If we could make someone else feel loved everyday, when our last thirty minutes does come, we will know we have lived our lives about as well as can be expected.

> Yesterday is history
> Tomorrow is a mystery
> But today is a gift
> That's why they call it the present.
>
> Time is too slow for those who wait
> Too swift for those who fear,
> Too long for those who grieve,
> Too short for those who rejoice.
> But for those who love, time is eternity.
> —Henry Van Dyke

Why?

There are things in this world I simply do not understand. I have questions.

For example:

- Why do grass seeds seek out, root themselves and flourish in a quarter inch of lifeless dust in a crack in my concrete driveway, and yet refuse to grow in the tended, fertilized bald spots in my lawn?
- Or why does the grass now thrive and struggle out from under the tons of rock we finally covered the side of the yard where previously grass absolutely would not grow?
- Why do weeds grow where flowering plants won't?
- Why is it that the price tags on flower pots, which are glued down with space age adhesive that takes nothing less than sand blasting to remove, are always in view no matter how many times I turn the pot?
- Why is it that price tags are glued down with space age adhesive that takes nothing less than sand blasting to remove?
- Why is it that price tags always cover the part of the label I really want to read?
- What is the real difference between scattered showers and isolated showers?
- Why is it that, while driving, when I desperately need to fish something out of my handbag, I cannot buy a red light, but on the day I am late for an appointment, I can't get a single green light?
- Why are drug companies allowed to spend millions of dollars advertising drugs to us, that we can neither buy or use without a presciption or even know what they are for in the first place and then pass on the cost of said advertising to us?
- Why are DVDs and CDs sealed up like state secrets?
- Why are some things, like certain razor blades and plastic electric toothbrush heads, locked up inside glass display cases as though they

were made of rare metal and I have to find an employee with a key to get to them?

• Why can't I find an employee at Home Depot or Lowe's when I really need one but ten of them will ask me if I need help, when I don't?

• Why is it that when I need to jot a quick note the only thing I can find to write with is a white crayon or a yellow highlighter or a pencil that needs sharpening?

• Why is it all pencils in the pencil cup need to be sharpened, always?

• Why does the inside of my car smell like the monkey house at the zoo?

• Why is it that no matter how I part my hair, the wind will blow it the opposite way?

• Why do I have to swear on the Bible in court when the Ten Commandments cannot be displayed in a federal building?

• Why is it that our children can't read a Bible in school, but they can in prison?

• Why do we only get to choose from just two people to run for president and fifty for Miss America?

• Why is it that a viable baby can be stabbed in the neck as long as it hasn't finished emerging from the womb, but it's murder for an unborn child to be killed during the commission of a crime?

Inquiring minds really do want to know.

In all affairs it's a healthy thing now and then to hang a question mark on the things you have long taken for granted.

—Bertrand Russell (1872 - 1970)

Boomertude

*B*orn near the center of 1947, I am an authentic, bone-fide, card-carrying Baby Boomer and I'm not ashamed to admit it. I say this because some Boomers hate the term, and angrily reject the label. This, of course, would be quite consistent with Boomertude. Firstly, real Boomers automatically rebuff labels; apparently it's in the unwritten by-laws. But secondly, and perhaps more importantly, the generation that adopted the slogan, "trust no one under thirty", presses on with fierce desperation, clinging to youth even as gravity and nature press back against us with inevitably greater force. Thus, you can thank Boomertude for making Botox, liposuction and tummy tucking as commonplace as teeth cleaning.

There is no effective way to explain Boomertude to the generation that birthed us or the generations we, in turn, launched. The children born between 1946 and 1960 know though. Boomertude was hardwired into us even before our first gasps and vocal cries of protest. The world, war-weary and exhausted by sacrifice, tired of despots trying to overpower and enslave us, was ripe for change, wide open for innovation, ready to get on with modern living and everything that this, as yet undefined, concept promised. Technology, first developed to contribute to the war effort, was quickly revamped to more commercial endeavors. Figuratively speaking, swords were cleverly hammered into plowshares, or more precisely, market shares. Without missing a beat, the gears shifted and commerce, not survival, was the engine thrusting civilization forward.

Entering the fifties, some bright marketing exec must have noticed a new demographic emerging and then quickly did the math. Overnight, the inordinately large number of babies and young children bursting into the population tables became a serious marketing focus. No surprise the scramble to rev up to this new paradigm left not a few traditions in its dust, such as the natural pecking order, for example. Suddenly, youth and everything to do with youth became the topic du jour and the one to pander to. Conversely, age, and its theretofore-revered accumulated wisdom, was summarily kicked aside. History reveals this to be a truly lucrative gamble for Wall Street, however, because fifty plus years down the road, Boomers still hold the record for being the most socio-economically influential demographic in recorded history. Tracking the progress of the Boomers is as easy as watching the evolution of commercials on TV. From the catchy jingles for sugarcoated cereals in 1955 to anti-aging cream in 2005, Boomers' interests continue to rule. In our defense, it's hard to be humble when all indicators point to the universe having been custom designed specifically for us.

All that said, there is something else, albeit less prominent than the development of the institutionalization of commercialism, for which Boomers will one day be credited. We originated the philosophy, if not the phrase, of thinking-out-of-the-box. My innate sense of Boomertude causes me to winch at that now hackneyed expression, but how better to say it? We didn't know we were thinking out of the box, of course. Actually, we didn't even know there was a box. We thought we were boldly stepping away from our parents' archaic way of doing things and reinventing the wheel, as does every new budding self-absorbed generation. What we didn't realize was the inevitable and certain impact of our massive numbers. Like all youths we thumbed our noses at convention but even in disorganization there is indeed influence by overwhelming quantity. When we questioned everything that smacked of authority, we established new trends that could not be quelled. We became the first American generation to roar, in unison, "no" to the establishment and for the first time the establishment was unable to defend itself against our volume. If our older siblings and/or parents were rebels without a cause, we would become rebels with good reason, we thought. Among other things we could not reconcile the first hand experience of our peers dying in a war that made no sense to us or the disparity in the lack of civil rights for certain segments of society. Instead we did what any out-of-the-box thinkers would do, we made ourselves heard. We protested, sat-in, marched, burned our draft cards, and dropped out in all the ways we could think of to escape the angst of the inequities of life, among these, co-existing with The Bomb. All the while we claimed to be the first generation smart enough to recognize and embrace our own alternate, drug induced realism. Make love not war, think globally, live locally. Greenpeace, Peace Corp, peace, peace, peace. We, in and by our newly devised wisdom, determined that peace and love was the answer to everything. Of course, pot helped some of us see this new vision with intense acuity.

And then there were the rest of us.

Supportive in spirit, albeit passively, the rest of us watched as these bold things, sit-ins, marches, protests, unfolded before us on the nightly news. We sang along with the politically charged music of the sixties and seventies, longing to be amongst the crowd at Woodstock. But instead we went to school, found jobs, got married and had families. Interestingly, as it turns out, Boomertude can work in a variety of ways. It can be just as effective as the impetus for founding a hippy commune as well as a multi-billion dollar computer software business. Boomertude is nothing if not versatile. It is tenacity, work-arounds, vision, blazing untried trails, regardless of risk. It is both diving in completely as well as stepping away totally. The one conundrum of Boomertude is the multiplicity of definitions and applications. One can still have Boomertude whether a laid back, 100% off-the-grid organic or a fully engaged stressed-out workaholic. But if Boomertude were a real word, one that could be looked up in the dictionary, regardless of the myriad of synonyms, the single antonym would be *victim*. Boomers are too independent and cynical to be victims. This is why predator marketers will find we won't be the easy marks our more gullible and trusting parents have been.

Unfortunately, Boomertude cannot be taught, like other philosophies, because to understand it one has to have been born into it. Into the era, the moment, that fleeting splash of light, like passing through the tail of a comet that will never return. To understand Boomertude, you have to already have it. Unfortunately the time for acquiring it is now passed.

Too bad.

Faith in the ER

My dear daughter-in-law, Halo (my nickname for her because she is an angel), called at 4 pm. My son had to drive to Virginia and she was alone and very ill. Fortunately, they live close so I could be at her side in less than fifteen minutes. She was suffering from the standard crud going around except that she had some unusual symptoms, like a feeling of numbness in her extremities which I thought needed looking at, even though I had quickly done a "mom" diagnosis of dehydration we decided to take her to the ER.

We arrived at the packed Gwinnett Hospital emergency room at 5 pm. It took an hour to even be called into triage so that the seriousness of her complaint could be determined and how far up or down on the list she would be allocated. Some poor souls had already been there for 5-1/2 hours. We waited along with dozens of other sick and hurting people. It occurred to me that the waiting room of the ER is a primordial soup of germs and viruses whose only reason for existence is to wipe out humanity. It also occurred to me that illness is a great leveler. Everyone, the rich, the poor, old and young were all there desperate for help.

Halo was just miserable and simply could not get comfortable in the hard chairs. At one point she sat on the floor and put her head in the seat of one. That is when I convinced her to lie down on two and put her head on my lap. Then I put my hand gently on her hot forehead and realized I could pray for her. Duh. Now, mind you, I certainly have the faith that God can and will heal us through righteous touch but I personally have never done it before. Anyway, I believed that if He willed for her to improve, she would, so I prayed in Christ's name for her illness to leave.

Twenty minutes later she sat up and looked at me and said, " I think I feel better. I'm not so achy. What if we go home and I'll just drink Gatorade and re-hydrate?"

Which is what we did.

Now, there are those who will be quick to conclude that she was already on the mend and that prayer or no prayer, hand or no hand, the outcome would have been the same. Others will see the value of believing in faith as a tool of healing. Regardless, what the experience did for me was to confirm something else.

In all the debating about the existence of God and the rationale of whether or not religious belief systems enhance or destroy civilization, there is always one thing overlooked. And ultimately it is the key to a higher understanding.

Many religions focus on living righteously, being good, honest, kind, loving and growing toward an elevated level of consciousness. This is not new. Seeking what is considered "good" as opposed to "bad" is generally accepted as what is best for the survival of mankind. Violence and greed, lasciviousness and wanton living often result in empty damaged lives. These are among the many vises considered "bad" and the fruit of such behavior is rarely worth plucking. Like in the parable of the withered fig, the tree that produced it should be destroyed. So, one way or another it is in our best interest to climb up at every opportunity rather than wallow in the mud. Common sense and desire for quality in life, not just religion should easily come to this conclusion.

Religion is the traditional vehicle to help with this struggle to reach for high ground and many successfully become new and better people through a belief system or organized doctrine; the fruit of which is peace, joy, and purposeful living which overlaps and spills over into other lives. Good begats good. Of course, many abuse and misinterpret dogma and generally speaking I find that these types don't really love anyone but themselves, which indicates that they didn't understand anyway. They didn't get it anymore than those who openly reject and actively argue against faith based living. Unfortunately, they still call themselves Christians and it is they who get the spotlight and give Christianity a bad image to those who eagerly seek to find reasons to debunk it.

Yes, people can be good without religion. Perfectly logical fleshly explanations can often be applied to otherwise tagged spiritual events. But it isn't so much the event as the fruit or result/purpose/outcome that is the key. It is the fruit of such things that many times cannot be explained away and sometimes is even hidden.

As we were driving home, Halo, who once again felt like talking said, "Thank you for putting your hand on my forehead. You prayed for me didn't you?" I said yes, I did. She replied that she knew it and smiled.

She also knew that she went from wishing someone would shoot her to feeling 100% better in a matter of minutes.

In this instance, the fruit born of the faith that prayer and touching could actually heal was better than medicine for her in that moment. Something in her was deeply nurtured and comforted by this. Medicine is only for the body anyway which is temporal. The health of the spirit will always take precedence over the importance of the flesh, but which can only come from a leap of faith.

For some it is unfathomable, for others it is a wisdom, nevertheless the fruit is real and undeniably good.

Now faith is assurance of [things] hoped for, a conviction of things not seen.

-2 Corinthians 11:1

Flaws

I never have time to watch daytime TV, but sometimes I turn the small one on in the kitchen to keep me company when I am working on recipes, usually tuned into the Food Channel. One day recently, I was otherwise focused on the problem at hand and looked up and realized the noise coming from the corner was not the Food Channel but rather a mid-day talk show. The topic was about women who had decided they were happily overweight and content with their size. That got my attention.

The featured women were individually showcased and one by one their personal stories were presented, each summing up their lifelong struggles and failures to lose weight. Each had come to the conclusion that the time had come to stop fretting over their dress size and move on to other more satisfying occupations of their time. The host, however, seemed intent on destroying their resolve and self-acceptance. His focus appeared more on bringing them back to his definition of reality. Oh, he was sympathetic and understanding but, once they were together on the stage he asked them all, "You say you are happy with the way you are, but if you had a foolproof way to lose the weight, would you?"

This pointed question put the ladies in an obviously compromised position. If they said yes, then they would have to admit that they were lying about accepting themselves as is. If they said no, they opened the door to ridicule. It pained me to see them struggle to find the words for an effective reply that would not put them on the defensive.

This is why I can't watch these kinds of shows. I get all frustrated because I instantly knew what their answer should be, but I couldn't crawl inside the TV and sit with them as their spokesperson. If I could have, this is what I would have said:

Yes, if there were a foolproof way for me to be thinner, I would. But mind you it wouldn't be for self-image. It would be more for making my

I Was Just Thinking

life in a *thin-worship* world easier because it would be the shortest distance between the two points of who I am and whom the world perceives me to be based on my appearance.

This is because, regardless of the political correctness of embracing diversity, we say we do, but we don't, not really. Are we uncomfortable when we pass someone who is noticeably disabled, do we avert our eyes? In a waiting room if there are two unoccupied chairs, one sitting next to someone who is fashionably thin or the other next to an overweight person, which do we choose? When the contestant on American Idol was told that she had a good voice but that she needed to lose weight, the judge was boo-ed by the audience. But I'd bet the farm that most people watching, even those who chided him, secretly agreed with him. Not that it was right, but because we have been conditioned to expect certain images as standard. Women, in particular, are expected to be shapely and thin first, with talented and intelligent tallying in as close seconds.

Like it or not, it is easier to be thin. Granted, obesity is not healthy, but for the most part the majority of us are not runway-model thin, anyway so what is this obsession with skinny? Why isn't it okay to be a size 14 or 16 instead of a size 4 or 6? I think the rationale is as complex as the human psyche. Thin represents self-control, fat speaks of gluttony. Thin is accepted as more intelligent, fat equates to slovenly and ignorant. Thin says, "I care about how I look," fat says, "I don't care". What is missing is all the pertinent truth, hiding underneath, that image alone can't tell us.

Being thin won't make life easier, but not being thin makes life twice as hard, absolutely. But a person's value should not be gauged by body size. I would have said this, if I had been there. I also might have thrown in that most of us are flawed in one way or another. How sad that those who are able to disguise their imperfections find acceptance far quicker than those who cannot. The counter-balance to this obviously tipped scale is that the most well-adjusted people are those who embrace their imperfections as assets rather than liabilities. Those who think in terms of self-worth based more in contributions to the greater good inspite of their flaws know the secret to a fulfilling life. Writers, artists, poets, statesmen, philosophers, volunteers, teachers, caregivers, ministers, the list is long for those who make a real difference in this world. They come in all shapes and sizes.

Amazingly enough, sometimes they are even thin.

On Death

I have attended two funerals in as many months. A funeral is a sobering experience, especially when you have been fortunate enough, as I, not to have been to one in over eleven years. It certainly makes you take stock. In December, the entire Buford Artists' colony was shocked into despair at the sudden death of Lee Bomhoff, a much loved, talented pastel artist. He was only thirty-nine. And yet with so much life left to live, Lee had already made such good use of the time he was granted here, his name was known around the world. His memorial service was packed with mourners and people who adored him. It wasn't just his talent, or his charitable works that endeared him to everyone who met him, more importantly, he was simply a good soul. He lived not just with good intentions, but with great intentions fulfilled. If there were nothing else to mention, for this he will be missed and long remembered.

I have wondered many times since his death which is better - to live a full, rich, giving life within the framework of less than forty years, or just to live long, self indulgently, never reaching out, never caring, always shielded with invisible armor, lest someone attempt to take advantage of you. Which is better, to be in control or to be flexible, to be right or to be gracious, to be selfless or self actualized, courageous or safe, to live nobly or covertly? And if integrity is doing the right thing even though no one else is looking, is it more important to quietly live honorably or to do what you can get away with and then put up a good front? What is your true worth, then? Perhaps more importantly, who could entrust you with confidences?

I'm not the least bit afraid of death, though I cling to life fiercely because I haven't done everything I have wanted to do yet, but I've been examining my life, thus far completed, with some haunting questions. It occurred to me, if I could imagine what my funeral would be like, could I look backwards from that point, like rewinding a video, and see myself

I Was Just Thinking

more objectively? And if I could, would I be able to make changes, like Scrooge who was allowed to see the old women pilfering his bed linens, laughing and making fun of his demise? If this concept makes you uncomfortable, then perhaps you should force yourself to rewind the video from the end also. You can never face too much truth for the truth is the only thing that makes us free and gives us second chances.

It might interest you to know that there is some form of The Golden Rule in nearly every religion, but, unfortunately, it isn't enough to know the Rule. If you don't practice it, your ability to feel genuine compassion begins to atrophy. It is blind compassion in general, that fine tunes the skill of forming true and intimate connections with others. And it is the intimate connecting that makes for strong marriages and lifelong friends, garners respect and affection and makes you worth loving. If you would be loved, warts and all, then it isn't enough to simply say you love, you must be willing to stretch yourself and care enough to explore what it is that makes another feel loved.

This, then, exercises The Golden Rule. To treat someone else the way you would want to be treated in return unconditionally. However, if you wake up every morning prepared to defend yourself from the slings and arrows of life, you will eventually be encased in a shell so impenetrable that you will be forever prevented from really experiencing personal, substantial, and rewarding relationships with other humans.

Is it not, after all, our ability to listen, to be sincerely compassionate, to be uplifting instead of negative, to encourage instead of discourage, and, lastly but not least, our willingness to be inconvenienced that makes us good parents, spouses, friends - and ultimately, good souls?

Lee must have known, somehow, what is important about living that makes death less final. For how can you really be gone, if you were worth remembering?

Death is more universal than life; everyone dies but not everyone lives.

-A. Sachs

Noise

Whatever happened to quiet?

Recently, while out of town on vacation, I was treating myself to a hairstyling. Seems I never have time for this simple grooming task unless I'm at least as far away as seven hours from my computer. The stylist I trusted my coifing to was recommended to me by my daughter so I took a chance and was looking forward to a brief encounter with a bit of pampering. The salon was upscale and interesting but for nearly an hour, while I sat having my hair sculpted, I was also having my brain cells rearranged by a relentless, thumping racket literally assaulting the room via four throbbing speakers.

These were positioned strategically in each corner, presumably to reach optimal auditory absorption. What it succeeded in doing was something akin to physical torture. After awhile, my stylist must have sensed my mounting discomfort because she stopped several times to try and change the selection on the stereo. It didn't work. Every number was the same. Same driving beat, same clanging, same eruptions by a nearly human voice droning repetitiously in some forgotten language. Finally, the stylist turned the stereo off completely. The silence was palpable. My deep sigh must have tipped her off that I had been approaching lift off. Our pact was unspoken, and for her intuition, not to mention a good cut, I tipped her generously.

Lately, I have become overly sensitive to the noise pumped through and into our environment and wonder why it has to be this way. Are we afraid to be alone in our own heads and who first figured out this dysfunction? When did it become necessary for us to have background music underneath everything we do? Doctor and dentist offices, car repair waiting rooms (although the insults there are mostly brain-numbing daytime talk shows) and even some grocery stores are now encapsulated in some kind of audible electronic stimulation.

Frankly, more than once I have simply turned around and exited a store that was filled to capacity with nerve-jangling din forced out supposedly as entertainment. Am I the only one who retreats without buying anything because the background music is holding my thought processes hostage? Allow me to insert here that I am a great music lover. I relish all sorts of music, from nearly every genre. And I use my home music system in parts of every day. I just don't need it going on twenty-four-seven. Here's an anomaly, I can even ride in my car without turning on the radio. Amazing, huh? What I am trying to say is, quiet is good. It is remarkable to me that just plain old silence has become a precious commodity in this overly wired world.

Unfortunately, piped-in music is not the only discord we endure. The other day, sitting in the airport, attempting to catch up on a little reading while I waited, I realized I had to read the same paragraph twice. Unsure of what was annoying me, I shifted in my seat and looked up to find on my left a young man banging away on his guitar accompanying himself as he practiced the same slurred lyrics and four chords over and over. Then I glanced up and discovered a TV suspended from the ceiling blaring a CNN broadcast. Added to the mix the computer at the airline check-in desk was relentlessly ticking and scratching out something. Suddenly, I noticed everything; the cacophony of the concourse in multiple layers. Babies crying over the low buzzing of hundreds of indiscernible conversations underneath announcements coming through the loud speakers at different gates, cell phones trilling, pagers chirping. I had to hold on to my seat for fear I might stand up and shout, "People, in the interest of sanity, we will now observe two minutes of silence!"

Instead, since it appeared I was the only one bothered by it all, I gave up and decided to seriously contemplate the noise pollution we are immersed in and accept without question, knowing it would result in a column. What I concluded was there is no escaping it. Even sitting on the porch in the evening the sounds emerging from the woods, the frogs and cicadas, can be loud enough to drown out quiet conversation. While at the beach I was delighted by the grand noise of the heavy-handed surf hammering away unmercifully at the beach. Though I understand this is labeled "white noise" to differentiate it from bothersome noise, I wonder why this is okay and promotes relaxation and the other noises of civilization seem to be at the root of stress and hypertension. I can't offer a definitive answer to this but I can make a guess.

For me, it comes to this, I can accept the natural noises, particularly those I have sought out. I like bird calls in the morning, even the sometimes obnoxious repetitive ones, when I'm sitting on the deck appreciating my first cup of coffee. I like the night noises, thick and complex, rising up out of the darkness. I like rain patting the roof and dripping from the gutter and the whooshing of leaves in the wind. I like thunder, whether it is the low grumbling type or the crashing attention-getting kind and the snap and sizzle of lightening. I like the gentle zuzzing of bees in the blooms of my Pink Gaura plants. I even like the creaking and groaning the dock makes when it's being bullied by the ever restless water. What I dislike is artificial noise that is arbitrary, altogether unnecessary, and forced on me. What I especially don't like is the assumption, made by people I don't even know, that I need some sort of programmed noise to keep me occupied. I am not afraid to be left to my own thoughts and internal resources while I shop, wait for appointments, ride in elevators and walk around in public places.

Am I the only one?

Like water which can clearly mirror the sky and trees only so long as its surface is undisturbed, the mind can only reflect the true image of the Self when it is tranquil and wholly relaxed.
 -Indra Devi - 20th Century Russian born American writer

I Was Just Thinking ~~~~~~~~~~~~~~~~~~~~~~~~~~~~~~~~~~~~~

Souvenirs

Some folks prefer mountains, others head to the desert, we are beach people. Vacation to us means, salt water, sand and pounding surf. Like all resort areas, most beach destinations are full of tourist traps packed floor to ceiling with all manner of trinkets and memorabilia stamped with the name of the locale so that years down the road, finding these otherwise useless things stored in boxes will instantly bring back all the good memories of that particular vacation. I have been known to buy a coffee mug in such a place, or maybe an extra towel or beach ball, but I have a much better way to preserve the memories of a family holiday.

A beach trip for me is not complete until we have done sand-casting. Smoothing out a small indention in moist sand, far enough away from the tidal line, and letting the kids press a foot or hand into the center, just deep enough to make an imprint. Then they can decorate with bits of shell, sea glass or drift wood, laid into the sand around the impression. I mix plaster of Paris in a small bucket with seawater and pour the creamy mixture into the impression, making sure the thickness of the plaster is about 1/2" deep. After it begins to set up, I cover the whole thing with dry sand and let it be for about an hour. It is a good idea to either put a child as a sentry to guard against someone running through and stepping into the middle of the hidden art or at least set a beach chair over it if no child can spare the hour.

Once the plaster is firm, I excavate it out of the sand, feeling much like an archeologist pulling up a chunk of ancient sculpture. It will be set but it takes about 72 hours for the plaster to cure completely and then the excess sand can be gently brushed away to reveal a perfectly preserved small foot or hand.

Some souvenirs can certainly recall the place but I think the best ones recall the people in the place.

The High Road

I recently had an opportunity to discuss the issue of the value of character-building and life choices in an online forum I belong to. It made me recall another discussion from years ago, when I had just dived into the online experience. One of my first forum involvements was in a woman's chat group. I was the newbie just trying to figure out how it all worked and so I rarely posted. I read mostly. But one day there was a rather sad plea for advice from one of the regulars. She said she was dying of cancer. She was married to a "nice guy" (her words) and had two beautiful (her words) teenaged daughters. Her dilemma was centered in the fact that she was in love with another woman. She wrestled with the decision to come out of the closet, risking devastating her family, especially her daughters, and live out the remainder of her days with the woman. She also tossed in the issue of insurance, which her husband provided for her through his employment and it was this insurance that paid for the expensive chemo treatments. Her question was, should she chuck everything, abandon her family and spend whatever time she had left with the woman she loved?

The responses were predictable. "Oh, you have to go with your heart!" "You owe it to yourself to do something for YOURSELF!"

Blah, blah, blah.

That tore it. I couldn't hold back. This is what I posted:

Most of our decisions in this life are pretty unremarkable and in the scheme of things we rarely have the definitive opportunity to make a choice that not only adds to our character but shines as an example of selflessness for those who follow us. How often do we get to consciously choose to do something that is better for someone else than it is for us? Facing exiting this life, regardless of what one thinks happens (or doesn't) after the last breath, one can still elect to leave a legacy of doing what is honorable and right over what is merely self-gratifying. Choosing the high road is never a mistake even if it means self-sacrifice and personal pain.

You might have guessed that I quickly experienced my first cyber-flaming as response to my post. In fact, I was chastised to a nice toasty crisp. They all jumped on me like vultures on roadkill. I discovered that I was insensitive and old fashioned. I was some kind of religious freak. I needed to come into the twentieth century. I should keep my narrow, mean-spirited point of view to myself. How dare I post such unbelievably cruel words?

Imagine that. Speaking to honorable action is now considered cruel words in this self-love society we live in. How did we get to this place?

I didn't hang around after that because I was pretty sure I would never be able to express my peculiar *old fashioned* POV on any issue after that so no need to waste any more time in there. I did always wonder what choice she ultimately had made. I'd have to guess that she is likely long gone by now. I had a feeling she probably didn't take the high road, though, and bequeathed to her nice guy husband and two young daughters a deep dark pain to deal with for the rest of their lives. And the truth is it would have been the same if it had been another man instead of a woman. Her choice was not about gender; it was about self.

Taking the high road is rarely easy, of course. The very nature of character enhancement is difficult or it wouldn't work. But what good is character in this case, you might ask? What good would it have done her? Once again, it wasn't about her at all. It was about those she left behind.

Taking the high road is about choosing to live well and to die even better.

The secret of a good life is to have the right loyalties and hold them in the right scale of values.

—Norman Thomas (1884 - 1968)

Fever

*F*ever can often make you see or think about minutia with skewed perspective. Heated brainwaves shimmer across the cosmic borderline between what is real and what is only perceived, the brief transition from the normal to the supernatural compelling imagination. Case in point, without the aid of an elevated temperature, I might never have considered the plight of the pin oak outside my window in the ivy bed.

She stands dwarfed by the tall leggy pines surrounding her, obviously ill suited to her spot, but with stoic grace even in the discomfort of her oddity. Clinging tenaciously to her dry coppery leaves until new buds push them and warm spring winds sweep them away, the pin oak is so unlike the other trees she must be an easy target for criticism and rebuke. Embracing diversity is not an inherent trait in nature and you rarely see the required self-discipline in a group mentality.

I know precisely how the pin oak must feel; the need for commonality but staunch belief in her true values. I'd offer up mediation with the pines if I thought they were evolved. But pines are somewhat shallow rooted and can only see from their higher vantage point. Anything other than the sharp verdant needles they share and staid comfort of their fixed and narrow standards must seem irrelevant and inconsequential to them.

Still in all, the pin oak doesn't seem to mind being the short deciduous tramp amongst the evergreens, the odd one out, the one who does things differently in spite of the distainful rushing whispers above her.

It's a pity actually. How can they see from their lofty heights that innovation was never born in status quo, never accomplished without risk of rejection and resistance? Their disregard for anything that challenges tradition as the archetype, sighting anomaly as being anathema to convention, the pines seal themselves off from original thought.

All things considered, I have to side with the pin oak, even if out of sync, than a pine arrogantly convinced of its own superiority.

Disadvantaged

    Disadvantaged. This word, like so many other overworked social adjectives, seems to have lost its original meaning. Since everything in today's culture boils down, in some way to money or the lack thereof, it has become synonymous with *poor*. My puppetry experience this past summer has given me pause to rethink this definition.

    Scheduled to perform, over the course of five weeks, in small, rural libraries, I had the opportunity to interact with a variety of children whose family income levels ran the gamut from near poverty to upper middle class. Guess which children made up the best audience?

    My first performance was in front of sixty-five children whose parents are primarily Hispanic immigrants who work in the poultry plants in and around Gainesville. Before I began I was warned by one of the librarians that the programs provided by the library and Hall County introduce most of these children to their first library experience. Her lowered tone of voice only added more tension to my already frayed nerves. My fears, however, were unfounded. The children filed in quietly, sat obediently, laughed appropriately, clapped loudly and made me feel completely appreciated. Whew! Not so bad. One down, four more to go.

    My next encounter was less encouraging but not a wash. My audience was made up of forty or so kids and parents from a nearby middle class suburb of Gainesville. They were less attentive and I can't remember if they clapped at the end or not. I was so glad to have even been able to finish because one two year old continually pushed his green truck into the face of the puppets while the mother visited with her friend. She finally noticed and then allowed him to walk behind the playboard to annoy me. Three more to go.

    The first two performances were in large conference rooms in shiny new libraries. Number three was in a tiny house converted to a library. Eight kids, four adults, including the librarian made up the audience of *less advantaged* rural people, but they responded with enthusiasm, and at least they clapped. Two sisters, aged twelve and eight helped me break down and load my stuff.

By the time I was setting up for my last performance I felt pretty much like a veteran. I had overcome the obstacles, one by one, with equanimity, including broken strings and spaces too small for my theater. My successes lulled me, I'm afraid, into a false sense of confidence. I didn't count on what the children of highly advantaged families could do to me.

Two hundred well-dressed kids and their caretakers, crowded into the big conference room of the new library. I had space, I had light, I had all my parts. I was excited that this, my last performance would be the best. I couldn't have been more wrong.

I couldn't see my audience, but I could hear them. They talked, laughed, argued, ran around and after the first scene I knew I was performing for no one. No adult told them to behave. No one suggested that the show be stopped until everyone was quiet, though I considered doing it myself. I decided to just keep going on, knowing no one was paying attention. Later, the librarian apologized and said these kids, who have everything, have literally no manners or appreciation for anything. She lamented that one mother calls each week to see what the program is going to be and then complains loudly if the librarian can't give her a synopsis. The fact that the programs are given free to the public seems irrelevant to this boor.

For me, the lesson is painfully clear here; the more we have and give to our children, the less they care about. I do puppetry to teach and share values as much as to entertain. I feel like a school teacher who must overcome the obstacles presented by those kids labeled *disadvantaged* before she can begin to teach. However, I have been challenged by the obstacles of kids who have every privilege and opportunity available for the basic requirements for normal development and who sneer at it, reject it and are then condoned by their parents, who are too busy making money so they can give their children more advantages.

I ask then who is truly disadvantaged?

Birthdays

*E*very year, around mid-May, friends and family ask me what I want for my birthday. In the past I have usually responded, "World peace." Frankly, given the sorry state of the world, I've rather given up on this lofty dream, so push coming to shove, I've devised a new answer.

I could use a clone/robot.

She/it needs to adore cleaning toilets and other grunt work. Her reaction to being told to mop the kitchen ideally will be fifteen seconds of clapping and yahooing. Furthermore, when told to sort/file/tidy my office, puddles of joy should glisten at the corners of her eyes. Yes, a clone/robot devoted to cleaning up behind me would be the perfect gift.

Unfortunately, we all know it's not going to happen anymore than homosapiens suddenly waking up loving and respecting each other. Outside of those two things I can't think of anything I need or want with the possible exception of a Clock-Stoppers watch. You know, the watch that speeds you up as the world inches along behind you. I'd take one of those.

You see, at fifty-seven, I've reached that place where people and time take precedence over things. I've got more jewelry than I could wear in two lifetimes, enough electronic devises and more kitchen gadgets than Emeril. Yes, I have plenty of things. But I do understand and appreciate the desire of those who love me to want to honor me with a physical something or other. I also am sympathetic with their plight at trying to find that perfect item that I might really want instead of wasting money on something I can't use. But what do you get for someone who has everything, anyway?

I feel their pain, I really do.

The truth is, gifts don't matter to me at all. Secretly, even as a child, I have always felt that my birthday was a genuinely special day that I share privately with God. It has been a day for me to reflect on where I've been, where I'm going and to quietly give thanks for my life and my blessings. It has also been the day I grant to myself, once a year, to do whatever seems right, with no guilt about dishes left unwashed, clothes heaped in a pile needing to be folded. It is a day for me, given by God.

On reflection, thinking about all the gifts I have ever been given, I know that the best was salvation anyway.

Not even a dish-washing clone could top that.

To divide one's life by years is of course to tumble into a trap set by our own arithmetic. The calendar consents to carry on its dull wall-existence by the arbitrary timetables we have drawn up in consultation with those permanent commuters, Earth and Sun. But we, unlike trees, need grow no annual rings.

- Cliff Fadiman

Morning

I am a morning person. And not just a morning person, I am an early morning person. This annoys some people. I'm sorry. I do try to be conscientious and not make noise while others might still be snoozing. I have a policy never to crank up any power tools or stereos before a reasonable hour. But it is in the early hours, when my energy level is high, I am clear headed enough to make my lists and then dive in. Though I am not a AAA personality type I still seem to have a certain ability to get things done, but ninety percent of this is accomplished before 3:00 p.m., at which time I begin to fade. I believe it is because I am propelled by the promises and potential of a new day. So, while others are still snoring, I am getting on with it. For those of you who will never see a sunrise, let me share a few things morning people, like I, might experience.

For one thing, if you are an early riser, quiet coffee on the porch while the deep mist of night is gently dissolving against pink- gold skies as the loons warn each other, puts the day ahead into a certain clear perspective. There's a peace and tranquility that no other part of the day can muster. These tender moments, fleeting but full of hope and encouragement, will always find me waiting respectfully. I have long talks with God here. I do the talking, I might add - He is a good listener even as He orchestrates the sunrise. Some early risers use this time to jog or do other forms of exercise. I appreciate that, but sometimes, I think exercising the spirit is as important and leads to better health. Plus you don't have to get all sweaty.

Fortunately, Ron is a morning person, also. Our radio alarm goes off at 5:00 a.m., which leads me to tell you about another thing late sleepers miss - O'Neil Williams' Great Outdoors Show on WSB 750 Radio. He is on from 4:00 - 6:00 a.m. Saturdays. Let me insert here that I love the outdoors but I have never been much on fishing and certainly not hunting. However, O'Neil is and he loves what he does so much...

"Welcome to another great unused Saturday morning!" He announces with genuine gusto. His wife "Woman Williams" is there with him, adding a touch of the feminine side to the subject matter. They take calls from other early morning people, talking with passion about spinner bait and frog colored chug bugs and reports on the best times, places and depths to try for the big one - that ten million dollar large mouth bass. Mostly, I don't have a clue what he is talking about but I completely share his joy. And though we are only half awake, Ron and I often laugh out loud at O'Neil's sometimes raucous good humor. When was the last time you started your day, laughing with your spouse? I tell you, nothing is more marriage fortifying than a mutual chuckle snuggled next to your sweetheart in the shadows of predawn. O'Neil will never know us, but we consider him a good friend - one of our early morning friends. Why, we'd even let him fish off our dock. He'd probably be interested to know that a trio of huge stripers often hang out there. I know this because I've seen them down there in the early morning, cruising silently like submarines in the shallows where the water is as smooth and glossy as patent leather.

Last but not least, I want to tell you what it feels like to make the turn east on Friendship Road from McEver at 7:15 a.m. and be confronted with, in its complete and awesome glory, a perfect, neon orange mid-November sun piercing through a thick, ambling ribbon of fog. And though the road disappeared into this spectacular scene, I drove forward, blinded, but with unwavering faith that the road was still there; all of my senses heightened from the unexpected, exquisite grandeur. As I turned south on Atlanta Highway, I was already committing this incredible ten seconds to long term memory. I'll take it with me into senility.

Joy comes in the strangest packages. We can miss it sometimes by being too busy to look.

Or by sleeping in.

Princess Ha-Ha

When she was nine years old her mother told her she was related to royalty. She believed it willingly and immediately embellished the concept because she wanted more than anything to be a princess. This wonderful secret gave her a delicious sense of power over her fourth grade peers who largely ignored her when they weren't teasing her. Her new perspective gave her the composure to smile serenely when picked last for kickball (though her lack of athletic abilities did, in fact, warrant this humiliation). And though she had always found adequate solace in her imaginary friends, the enlightenment of her true royal self became a deep wellspring of strength. Insulated by this armor, she could hold her head up high, no matter what indignity the world might try to inflict.

For several months into the school year, she was quite content to live the regal, solitary life of a long lost blueblood, until, one day, when the superior person of Miss Margaret Cooper made a disparaging remark about homemade dresses. As the damning words escaped her mouth, the scrawny, blonde urchin, dressed in a handcrafted blue gingham dress, watched herself, as though out of body, tell her tormenter that she obviously didn't know she was making fun of a real princess whose lineage reached across the ocean to the English throne.

For an instant, Margaret's blank expression offered hope that the words had been believed, or better yet, not heard at all. And then, Margaret Cooper turned on her patent leather heels, hailed down the nearest infidels and, as the horrified wannabe princess watched helplessly from behind a lanky Texas pine, spilled the treasured secret out like dirty mop water on the dusty playground. By the time the task was complete, the entire fourth grade was fully informed that the least one among their ranks believed she was a princess. This included the teacher, Mr. Blackman, who had, by chance, just recently notified her mother, "she daydreams too much". Mr. Blackman, being less than sympathetic with the delicate nature of the nine-year old psyche, promptly made a joke of the whole thing by bestowing on her, like a crown of thorns, the title, "Princess Ha-Ha".

A lesson hard earned is a lesson well learned. And though it took several years to live down her new nickname, she would never forget the first rule of royalty- which is: never, ever, no matter how persistent they are, let the Margaret Coopers of the world get past your royal guard.

If you reveal your secrets to the wind you should not blame the wind for revealing them to the trees.
-Kahlil Gibran (1883 - 1931)

Time

*R*ecently, during casual conversation, lingering at the table after a delicious meal, the challenge was issued to name our top five favorite movies. I asked if we were talking pre WWII or post? Nope, just the top favorite all-time-no-qualifiers-allowed movies. Even as bad as the film industry has declined over the years, if you take a minute to think about it, you will discover, as we did, how difficult this is.

Five is a small number when you are using it to rank hundreds, maybe thousands of flicks. I was the first to announce my top five, although I know the list would change if ever I was asked this again. But for the sake of not drifting off to sleep from too much food and the lull in the conversation, I said, number five, the first William Powell Thin Man movie, number four, The first Pink Panther movie, number three, Raising Arizona, number two, Mr. Holland's Opus and my all time favorite movie that I could see once a week is Ground Hog Day.

To my surprise, my choices initiated animated rebuttal. It seems there are serious camp divisions over Raising Arizona and just like coconut, you either really like it or you really don't. But everyone generally agreed that Ground Hog Day was a good choice, if maybe not for the blue ribbon position. Then, I was forced to consider why Ground Hog Day, certainly not an Academy Award candidate, made it to my number one slot. Well, yeah, Bill Murray is a great comic performer and you can truly get into his characters. But I'm thinking the part could have been played by others equally as well. Tom Hanks, for example. And then, of course, I did love the setting in a small town; this is always a winner for me. But, overall, the real reason I love this movie is the whole concept of having absolutely all the time you need to do whatever you want. Furthermore, there's the hook that reels you into the storyline.

The guy is such a jerk and before it is over he has learned all the valuable lessons of life, while he still has the rest of his life to use them. Now that's

I Was Just Thinking

one you can file under "never happens in real life". And that's what makes the whole thing so appealing. Not only does it feed into my insatiable need to have more time to do what I want to do, it also allows me to wallow in the fantasy of getting my lessons early on so I can just spend the rest of my life basking in wisdom and reaping the rewards of good choices and righteous living.

So, that's it then. The crux of the matter is not only about having enough time to learn how to speak another language or play an instrument. It is more about graduating quickly and getting on with life, armed with good character, depth, compassion, patience, sincerity, honesty, and a high emotional IQ. The remaining journey down the yellow brick road would have to be less difficult with all those skills tucked inside your tote.

Right?

Alas, life is not a movie. And while life occasionally imitates art, the tote we start with is pretty much empty. It's all the troubles and near misses we encounter on the way that help us begin to fill it up. And unlike the illusion of the movies, we are indeed lucky if we "get it right" before we hit the last scene of the final act.

Unfortunately, being real instead of fictional characters, more often than not, we pick up the wrong lessons along the way like bitterness, pettiness, revengefulness, jealousy, self-pity and self-centeredness. And when our final credits roll, it's too late. Fini. The End. Time's up. No reruns.

Too bad life can't be a movie, huh?

Time flies like an arrow. Fruit flies like a banana.
-Groucho Marx (1890 - 1977)

What I Need...

I'm standing in line at the grocery store. I chose this line because the lady in front of me was nearly checked out and then she forks over a fistful of coupons to the clerk. The clerk groans a little and seeing it's going to be a while, I start reading the headlines on the tabloids. Same old, same old. I peruse the ladies mags and my eye falls on a tempting cover featuring a beautiful holiday pie. It is perfect, mint green, festooned with whipped cream and colorful little handmade marzipan packages, each tied up with slender piped ribbons of chocolate.

Suddenly I feel an overwhelming sense of inadequacy. I have this vision of me slaving over this pie all day and then presenting it with practiced grace and humility to a gathering of friends and family. I accept with aplomb the accolades and generous ohs and ahs. How do you do it? You made this yourself? I drift into the memory of an old neighbor and domestic rival, Marva, who seemed to believe we were in some sort of life competition with each other. I could see her stewing behind a sweet smile, "Who does she think she is, Martha Stewart?" Letting Marva into my reverie bursts the bubble. Who am I kidding? I have never had time to make tiny marzipan packages to put on top of a perfect pie that I couldn't make anyway. This is when the inadequacy thing kicks in. To top it off I'm annoyed by the fact the lady in front of me has so many coupons the clerk owes her money. This is the last straw. I need to take some kind of action. I need to get some control over this hectic life I lead.

Here's my plan - an ad in the paper for a detail person.

I need a detail person. I go home and carefully compose this:

W   a   n   t   e   d

I Was Just Thinking

Detail person. Duties include but are not confined to, perfect pie making (marzipan art desirable but not required), coupon cutting, filing and remembering where you put them, Christmas card writing, and stamping and mailing, refrigerator cleaning, baseboard dusting, plant watering, magazine reading and throwing away, checkbook balancing, neighborhood coffee club attending, romance novel reading, handmade Christmas gift making, purse cleaning, social telephone call returning, 100% cotton clothes ironing, afternoon nap taking, computer dusting and automobile oil changing. If you think you are the person I need, please send resume.

I wish I had thought of this years ago. What I would have given to have seen Marva's face when my Christmas decorations went up before Christmas and down before Valentine's Day.

I quit therapy because my analyst was trying to help me behind my back.

—Richard Lewis

66

Faith is a Verb

July 10, 1956

The tear soaked words of the radio preacher floods into the room, drenching the listening woman and child with desperation. The child looks up at her mother and asks, "Why is he crying?"

"He needs money to keep his radio ministry on the air." The mother answers without a pause from the task at hand. Four crisp white shirts hang behind her on a hook. One remains in a moistened ball, like sculptor's clay, waiting for its turn to be transformed. The sixth shirt, draped over the creaking ironing board, submits itself without a fight to the deft experience of the woman's hand and the steaming heat of the iron.

"Why doesn't he just use his time to preach about Jesus and let God send him the money?" asks the child, focused on keeping her red crayon marks from straying outside the lines on the coloring book page. She does not notice her mother's stunned face looking down at her nine-year old daughter.

"Out of the mouths of babes," the woman whispers.

The child looks up to find her mother's astonished smile beaming back at her.

"You're pretty smart, young lady, maybe you should write Brother Roloff a letter."

"What would I say? I'm just a kid. Why would he listen to me?"

December 17, 2004

The woman types the last of the labels and hits the print command. She looks up at the small TV screen and turns up the volume with the remote. "What you have here," the evangelist says, "is an opportunity to finance the end time harvest. We are attempting to get a new satellite into orbit that will broadcast the gospel twenty-four hours a day, seven days a week to the Middle East. Dollars equals souls," he continues, "Dollars equals souls." Another man in the background, excited over this new catch phrase echoes his agreement, and enthusiasm, "yes, yes, amen, dollars equals souls."

With the click of the remote, the screen goes black and silent.

Nothing new, under the sun. I should write a letter, the woman thinks to herself, Or not... She turns to respond to the email messenger's ping, opens it and reads.

dear sister in Christ, i have received the book so fast thanks- i would like to give a small donation on line via credit card. please advise. i am halfway reading the book and it has blessed me so far. i am going through a lot recently with no job and anxious about my next mortgage payment plus i am recovering from respiratory infection. the book is such a blessing to me. I understand what's in the book i just have to put in practice. again thanks and God bless please say a prayer for me and don't forget to email me with the website i can give on line donation to you and if you have it...

The woman closes her eyes and exhales slowly, praying to find the best words to respond. After a moment she types,

Dear, sister, I understand that you want to give something, but I do not believe God wishes for you to go into debt, especially since you are unemployed. There are many things you can do that do not involve using your credit card. I am guessing that you know someone else who needs comfort or time or prayer. God provides funds for this ministry by those whom He appoints. He calls us all to give but only that which we are able. He has all the money He needs. What He wants more is willing, humble hearts. Dollars don't equal souls, laborers, and the word of God equal souls. Jesus said He needed laborers, the faithful who are willing to sacrifice of themselves, to lay aside their plans for this life, and offer their all to the pursuit of furthering the Kingdom of God. When Jesus sent out the seventy disciples, He commanded them to carry neither moneybag, sack, nor sandals. All they had was Christ's word, and that was enough for them to go and preach the gospel. Trust and obey and you will know where you can help.

Her finger hovers over the send button long enough for her to ask that the message be blessed and then she taps it. "Lord," she asks, "how do I make them understand? Who am I that they should they listen to me?"

The woman prepares two heavy boxes and five smaller packages with the shipping labels and loads them into her trunk. As she drives to the post office she hears the words echoing in her head, carry neither moneybag, sack, nor sandals. She wonders if there is more to faith than simply trusting the unknown.

"You must have had a plan, Father, bigger than we give you credit for," she prays out loud. "As members of The Body, regardless of our trials or troubles, we must each have something to contribute to the whole, regardless how small it seems to us. Is it faith that finds the truth of this, or truth that calls faith to the quest?"

The woman struggles to enter the building with her heavy boxes and packages when a knobby, wrinkled hand reaches around her to hold the door. "Oh, thank you so much," she turns to give her assistant a smile. The frayed around the edges elder, flashing a near toothless grin, replies, "Looks like you could use some help, dear."

"Yes, I could, for sure. And then you come along. You must be an angel."

"Oh, at's a new one, never been called an angel afore." The old man's weathered face brightens as if a light has clicked on.

"Well maybe no one has ever seen you like God sees you."

The pair wrestles the heavy burdens into the post office to wait in the long line. When the old man takes his turn at the counter, he can't find the change he needs to buy his stamps. Frustrated and embarrassed he fumbles in his pockets. The woman steps up and gives him a twenty dollar bill. "Looks like you could use some help, dear," she pats him on his fragile boney shoulders.

"Now, who's the angel?" His rheumy eyes threaten to spill over with the salty waters of gratitude.

"Nah, no angel," she says.

Before she leaves the post office, the woman opens her PO Box and finds two envelopes. One contains nothing but a twenty dollar bill wrapped in plain paper. The other yields a money order for three hundred dollars and a note of praise.

On the way home the woman hears, "You do not need to tell them, show them."

Aging

After a long hard Saturday of cleaning and preparing and then a Sunday hosting our annual Kick-The-Season-Off-Dock-Day, Monday, Memorial Day, 2004, was definitely a day to rest. Our old policy of *a day to prepare, a day to enjoy and a day to recover* takes on new meaning for us each year as the preparing part and the enjoying part becomes more challenging, making the recovering part even more and more necessary.

Aging is a cruel joke. Just as you are old enough to know some important things and figure out what you want from life, you're too tired to do it. Well, I'm not laughing.

But Monday morning we slept in, awakened by a wonderful hardy rain drumming rhythmically on the roof. It was an invitation. Most of the day I spent on the screen porch embedded in the glider cushions reading. Ron came out for a while and we sat in devout silence. It was one of those profound pauses in time that often come at the conclusion of frenzy. I felt compelled to grope for a word that would best describe how I was feeling about having a gloriously unstructured day, as though that definition might have a more medicinal effect. All I could come up with was "repair".

I was staring out mindlessly toward the back garden and the lake beyond and my eye refocused in on the bouquet of gardenia blooms sitting in front of me. I had rescued the fragrant blossoms earlier from sure rain damage and stuck them in a plastic cup of water, a leftover from the previous day's festivities. The thing that caught my eye was a sparkle of light on one perfect drop of rain hanging tenaciously to the tip of a creamy petal. I told Ron to be still, afraid that any movement might cause the droplet to fall. I eased up, careful not to bump the table, and slipped away to find my camera. As I was sprinting up the stairs two at a time, I told myself this effort was futile and the drop would be gone before I could return to capture it. But it was still there and I got my shot.

Afterward my thoughts wandered off to examine this whole aging thing. I was feeling much like the raindrop, hanging on precariously by nothing more than surface tension. I was so tired I could hardly move, let alone dash up the stairs to retrieve my camera from my office at the other end of this house that seems to grow as I get older. So, where did that burst of energy come from?

I concluded that I have plenty of mental and spiritual energy remaining; it's just that my decaying body is letting me down. The slow decline that we experience as we grow older lulls us away from certain activities by small degrees until one day we realize we simply cannot do what we used to do. Since our hearts and minds are still raring to go, this comes as something of a shock as though it happened over night. If we aren't mentally prepared to give up the physical things we no longer have the oomph to handle, we are often left thinking we are done altogether. But this isn't true; we are not done. We are merely in transition.

Again.

Life, it turns out, is primarily a series of transitions. From birth to death we change. Sometimes we think we have to hang on. Sometimes we cling stubbornly to what was, like the rain droplet because we don't want to go to the next stage. Mostly we are only afraid of the unknown. But every stage of life has its rewards if we are willing to look for them.

I took a picture of the droplet on the gardenia petal and now, as a photograph, it is a visual work of art that can represent all that was excellent about that single moment in time. Unfortunately we can't do that with our lives. We have to make each moment singularly worthy. We cannot cling to what was and still have enough energy to make something great out of what is. The rule is: we have to let go before we can move on to the next stage even though we might be in a state of freefall for a time.

Accepting when it is the right moment to let go of one place in life to make way for the next is the hardest lesson of all but the one we must learn if we want to make the most of who and what we were meant to be in the time we are allotted.

That was the original goal wasn't it?

Kudzu Rules

*H*ere in the south, everyone knows about kudzu. It is a pest, a vine that, once established, is virtually impossible to eradicate. It climbs relentlessly over other vegetation in its innocent self-actualizing quest to survive; engulfing the host and blocking the life giving sunlight. Ultimately it can asphyxiate even the tallest, hardiest tree.

Most southerners are familiar with its history. It was imported in the 1800's from Asia by agriculturalists to prevent soil erosion. It seemed a good idea, then. But time often proves that occasionally even the best of intentions can turn sour. Unfortunately, kudzu is now entrenched and as much a part of the landscape as dogwoods and azaleas. Truth to tell, it isn't all bad. In the orient, the root is used to make a high grade, nutritious tofu and the thick woody vines are excellent materials for constructing beautiful baskets. But for the most part, there is no way around it, kudzu is insidious.

I see kudzu as a perfect analogy. Like so many other good intentioned attempts to advance our civilization, Kudzu Rules have slowly taken over and are choking out what was initiated as simple human fairness. Like kudzu, the idea that to survive and succeed we must conquer and use others, rejecting integrity, honor, and selflessness, grows mindlessly and with such speed, the deeply rooted values on which this country was founded are literally withering from lack of light.

In a sincere effort, thinly disguised as promoting human equality, we, as a nation, at the close of the second millenium, are now subject to lowest-common-denominator syndrome. Creeping upward in subtle increments, slowly surrounding and binding us, our beliefs about what is expected of us as human beings are gently smothered and replaced with the deep green, leathery leaves of lack of accountability. The tendrils of self-gratification and ego, questing for more room to grow, reach ever upward. Unfortunately we don't see it happening on a day to day basis.

In case you have been too busy to notice, here are the new

Kudzu Rules of Society:

- Self first. Serve your self. Make yourself happy first.
- Be offended easily. Be quick to defend your position. Shoot if you feel your position or space is threatened. Lie if it protects or advances your position.
- Never lift anyone else up, it might temporarily dislodge you from your position.
- Steal if you can't have what someone else has. After all, society will defend you because you are disadvantaged.
- Don't ever blame yourself for your bad decisions. Someone else is always available for that, especially your parents.
- Choose self-fulfillment. If you are struggling with the choice of living and dying nobly or self-fulfilled. Others can take care of themselves.
- You are what matters. Remember, no matter how little effort you exert, you are as good as anyone else and deserve everything anyone else has. If you need therapy for your confusion, the new professionals (with the exception of Dr. Laura) will encourage you to realize yourself, create and cultivate your self-esteem at all costs.
- Redefine compassion as "doing for" instead of "teaching to do".
- Squelch independent thinking whenever possible. Recognition of innovative ideas threatens the self-esteem of underachievers.

If you are an antique, like I, from the old school of thought, you are likely distressed, as I, by this inch by inch strangulation of what is civil about civilization. I truly feel sorry for all the hapless pupils of the new school who will never understand what hit them when the last ray of sunlight disappears.

Even kudzu needs something solid to grow on.

Everyone thinks of changing the world, but no one thinks of changing himself.
—Leo Tolstoy (1828 - 1910)

Old Friends

*N*ot once but twice recently I have had something from my past come back to me and even on the same day. Though I know you can't go home again, as the poet once penned, apparently it isn't impossible to revisit.

All on one day, I not only held my guitar and strummed the old dead strings, which prompted me to go get it cleaned up and outfitted with new ones, I heard from a dear friend that has been lost to me for nearly two decades. Both of these old comrades reentered my life so suddenly that it caused memories to tumble back as though they had been huge rocks pushed down a steep hill. I didn't even have time to dodge. The irony that confounds me is that my guitar playing days and my friendship with Cyndy were from the same era of my youth, both of which were responsible for giving me comfort in a time when I really needed it. I didn't even realize how much I had missed my girl friend and my guitar until I heard them both again. Sound is an amazing thing. There is nothing better than the clean ring of new guitar strings with the exception of the laughter of a long lost friend.

I started playing guitar when my two youngest kids were babies. I desperately needed something creative for myself besides changing diapers, washing dishes and running after toddlers all day. So, instead of folding clothes while they were taking their afternoon naps, I sat on the floor in the living room and taught myself how to play. I used a Mel Bay chord book at first and then progressed to a John Denver Song Book (Easy). It was a slow process but one chord at a time, one hour upon another, day after day, I learned to make simple music that I now attribute to having maintained my sanity during those manic years. Plus, eventually, I made a little extra grocery money by teaching kids basic guitar in my home after school several days a week. Though I never learned to play well, I learned enough to satisfy that needed balance between the spirit-killing drudgery of daily life maintenance and the soul-lifting creativity of music making.

Cyndy and I met through our husbands. On our first casual encounter we didn't try to become best friends immediately and stuck to safe generic conversations about children and potty training and homemaking in general. I don't recall the first time we realized we could open up to each other, share confidences and bond in a way that only women know how to do, but from that moment, Cyndy and I depended on each other for the support and strength it was going to take to get us through the years just ahead of both of us. We didn't know it at the time, of course, but in retrospect our friendship was an obvious blessing. One for which I will always be grateful.

Catching up with someone you haven't spoken to in seventeen years is not as hard as you might think. It's not unlike placing your fingers on the guitar frets to make chords that you thought you had forgotten and discover you haven't. First you find out about the kids and where they are and how many kids they have and what kind. You get the basics out of the way. Work? Marriage? Moves? And while the familiar voice and distinctive laughter is rummaging around in the back files of your memory, your mind's eye is pulling up images that you know must be long out of date. Regrettably you also know your own image needs updating somewhat, as well. Then you wonder if you really want to see what time has done to your friend or if you want her to see what it has done to you. Then you know it just wouldn't matter to either of you.

This has left me wondering. How do we let go of people and things that were once so important to us? We move, we change, our interests and circumstances shift, but not even decades can erase what once was. Years invested should not be filed away and abandoned. They should be recalled and enjoyed often. They are treasures, perhaps the only real riches we can claim in this life. The years and distance cannot change what we have spent so much time learning about and loving and that contributed significantly to shape whom we have become. Old friends should not be forgotten.

Should auld acquaintance be forgot, And auld lang syne! For auld lang syne, my dear, For auld lang syne, We'll take a cup o' kindness yet, For auld lang syne.

The Dish

He did it anyway. Against my objections, which were numerous and mostly valid, I might add, my husband installed - "The Dish". We are now directly linked to space. I tell you it's a scary thought. Naturally, in any life altering circumstance, there is always an adjustment period, but I'm not so sure I'll fully recover from this one.

For one thing, now we have yet another remote control to learn and keep track of. This makes four. Makes me start hyperventilating just to think about it. You see, I've never been especially adaptable to these electronic things. I know just enough about my computer to be somewhat dangerous and I did finally learn how to correct the time on the microwave after the electric has blinked off, but I will never learn how to use a VCR; this is a given. There's serious blockage in my learning receptors in this area. Lord knows I've tried. I know my husband thinks I'm just resisting.

And, truth to tell, he's right, but so what. I, at least, know where the on/off button is on the TV and don't even need the remote. He, on the other hand, will turn the room upside down looking for the always misplaced, pesky thing, missing a whole program during the search. Furthermore, I know how to select a program and then just watch it. He, however, will spend the first fifteen minutes, of any time-slot, channel surfing to see if there might possibly be something better. It's a male thing, I know. I've read it has to do with testosterone levels.

And, of course, with *The Dish* we have many more choices - not necessarily choices to watch, mind you, but choices to read about if we should wish to purchase them separately, above and beyond the monthly fee. So now, I venture to say, we spend much more time reading about what we could watch than actually watching anything. Did you know there are nineteen different all sports channels? Boggles the mind. To top it off, we still have cable because I didn't want to feel like I was out of town every time I watched the news. So, this gives us even more choices. I believe I read somewhere there are medical studies in progress that link too many choices with migraine headaches.

I do enjoy The Learning Channel and The History channel. I'll concede this. But these gains are hard to weigh against the dreaded weekend illness known as Movie Overdose - the symptoms of which are stiff back and joints and blank, vacuous staring.

Maybe this will eventually pass and we'll finally be able to strike a happy balance between Digital World and real life. I hope so. Longer days and warm weather are coming, thank Heaven. In the mean time, I guess I'll just have to find better hiding places for that darn remote.

Technology is dominated by two types of people: those who understand what they do not manage, and those who manage what they do not understand.

—Putt's Law

Weeds

*M*y favorite time to pull weeds is when it's drizzling. Not storming, mind you, but gentle, windless, straight down raining. Recently, in a steady downpour, I spent about an hour in my garden, plucking weeds that slurped up, right out of the saturated ground, roots and all, without the usual fight. It's quite gratifying, not to mention way easier. Gardening in the rain yields a number of surprising benefits because is a tactile experience, as well. For one thing there is the wonderfully therapeutic and aromatic earthy fragrance of rain dampened soil. There's also the life-affirming prick of raindrops on your face and the musical tinkle and pat of water hitting leaves while everything is bathed in the pale, surreal sunlight diffused behind cloud cover.

These heightened sensory pleasures, alone, are certainly worth the getting drenched, but I discovered there's something else worthwhile about working out in the rain, jog suit soaked, flattened hair dripping, sans makeup. There's a truth to be embraced but you have to be willing to step out with complete disregard for what it will do to your appearance. You have to temporarily compromise your adulthood and remember what it is like to be guileless as a child again. You have set aside the mild discomfort of being soggy and disheveled and let go of your self-pride and reason.

The secret benefit of weeding on a rainy day is learning that the best time, as well, to yank weeds from our hearts is when we are sodden with troubled waters. The analogy is perfect, is it not? Reduced to our least attractive, bedraggled selves, at the mercy of what a deluge can do to us, allows us a glimpse of what we must look like to God. No pretense, no façade, no way to hide behind artificial glamour or cool sophisticated intelligence, just the real us, vulnerable and in need of a big absorbent towel and a warm hug. But if we could but stop and compare the similarities between weeds in the garden and weeds of sin that flourish in our hearts and how much easier weeds are to pull when their resistance is softened, we could seize the moment and prune out a few, like jealousy, resentment or lack of charity. In that moment when we have been humbled and softened, we find our best opportunity. In this context, just as rain is a blessing, so can adversity be also, but if we are to take full advantage of the blessing we have to ignore the distress and be open to the good things that are doable in spite of or because of the distress. Life is a series of loosely linked possibilities, opportunities and mysteries to be discovered and unlocked. Sometimes these are disguised as rain.

The lessons abound for those who wish to step outside of convention, like seeing a rainy day as the perfect time to do a little weeding.

A man's children and his garden both reflect the amount of weeding done during the growing season.

—Anon

Child's Play

It's Tuesday. August is barely a week old. The kids and I are swimming at the dock. Though we have done this quite a bit this summer, today we do it with an edge of urgency. Like thirsty towels, we are soaking up as much summer as we can hold. Next week school starts.

Of course, we realize that summer isn't over just because the old regimentation has begun. There are still opportunities for swimming and other hot weather activities. After all, it doesn't really get cold until late in the fall, at least not here in the deep south, anyway. But without speaking of it, we know in our hearts, this is really the end of "our" summer. Our summer here at Camp Meema, that is. To console ourselves, we have discussed how much there will be to write about when the teacher assigns the dreaded "What I Did On My Summer Vacation" essay. A couple of beach trips, numerous movies, Six Flags, several museums, sleeping late, and slurping our weight in ice cream and watermelon. Hours spent playing Lake Monster and the Island of Doom ranks high, as well (they always believe they can out swim me, little fools!)

And then there was THE PROJECT.

We always do a summer project. This year it was pretty ambitious, even for us experienced summer project engineers. We built the By-The-Sea Beanie Bed & Breakfast. I'm not sure where the initial idea emerged from, but it blossomed quickly into a major undertaking that took us from the end of June and through all of July and into August. I built the main structure, of course, but the kids painted the rooms and all the furniture. They also made the hot dogs and the bags of peanuts, pretzels and tubes of suntan lotion out of Sculpey, for the Beach Bum Snack Hut. Hayes is quite proud to take credit for the terrific hot dog painted on the sign. Olivia learned some very nice scissor techniques while cutting out the beach towels. Dylan did a slam bang job both on room 401 and the chair and bunk bed. Even Meagan, though only five, proved she could paint with the best, with only the tiniest smudge of pink regrettably transferred to her shirt and just a tad in her hair.

Then one thing led to another.

Just when we thought we were done, we decided we needed a beach, after all, it is a By-The-Sea resort. We painted an ocean and sand on a large canvas. Hayes added an ominous gray fin in the farthest corner and then, as a precautionary after thought, decided to paint in a shark fence. Olivia painted the lifeguard seat and the stools for the Snack Hut. One day Carly was here by herself and she and I did a head count and decided we needed a couple more Beanies. We went gleefully on a Beanie hunt until we found just the right ones.

Then we played.

I know what you are thinking, especially if you are of the masculine persuasion. Good grief, the woman's got the boys playing with a dollhouse! But wait. Besides the fact that it isn't a dollhouse as much as it is a business replica, this project had some amazing benefits, both obvious and not so obvious. Some interesting lessons were learned along the way, both for the kids and for me.

First and foremost, we learned about setting a goal and working toward the conclusion a little at a time. We never said we couldn't do it, so we always believed we would. Hayes discovered the process of failing and then starting over when he painted the hot dog sign. He could see it in his head, but it wasn't turning out like he wanted it in the first try, so he crumpled in a heap of frustration until I reminded him that all artists work from sketches and trial and error until they get the results they want. It took a few tries, but in the end, he was amazed at himself and his final artwork. It looked exactly as he had visualized it. Olivia learned that sanding the cut ends of the wood is an art form in itself. Plus it is tedious but you do it to make the finished project equal to your effort. A job well done is a job well earned. Or something like that.

And there were other more subtle lessons. One day, after the kids left, I did a quick inventory of the B&B. I then went to the computer and typed up the following message:

Housekeeping has notified the front desk that there is a blanket missing in this guestroom. Please return the item to its proper place. Beach towels are available at the Beach Bum Snack Hut. Thank you, Specs, Manager.

I Was Just Thinking

The next day, Hayes found the note on the bunk in room 402. I was lurking to see what his reaction would be. His eyes widened, he started laughing and then he quickly went and found the blanket. Nothing has turned up missing since. I'm accepting this to mean a heightened sense of responsibility has now sneaked in the back door.

Friday, on our really final last day of Camp Meema, we are having a Concert On The Beach. We picked out some music and made a tape. With apologies to Jackson Browne, Celine Dion, Mary Chapin Carpenter and Chris Rice, we will be performing to the rest of the Beanies as they lounge on the Beach. A special stage was erected for the occasion. It sort of floats on the canvas water.

While we were brainstorming about this, it occurred to me that kids have unlimited potential while practicing life. It is this kind of open-ended pretending that teaches the problem solving skills humans need before stepping out into real life situations. And more than that it is the confidence that anything is possible that supports it all underneath, like a hidden raft. These are the real lessons here. If our children never have the time to pretend and to invent and create what was not, then what will become of us down the road? Toys that do all the thinking and leave nothing to the imagination are worse than sugar water. They have no benefits beyond the moment of consumption. This is a sobering thought because so many of the electronic games and the plethora of battery operated gadgets that line the shelves of toy departments, give nothing of real value back for the effort. Thumb exercising, is about all. Practicing life takes fertile imaginations but fertile imaginations come only from practice.

Next year, the kids have already decided we need a Beanie Restaurant and some cars. We'll do some sketches first. I have no doubt we will accomplish these things. How hard can it be?

And you know, we thought we were just having fun. Imagine that.

Those who say it cannot be done should not interrupt the one doing it.

—Chinese Proverb

Dad

I think about my dad on Father's Day. He died in 1979. For most of his life, he worked six days a week, ten hours a day, selling men's shoes. When I was a child, in Houston, he rode a bus to town and home again, leaving the family car for my mother to use. On Sundays, his only day off, he took us to church in the morning, then, after lunch, spent the early afternoon cutting the thick St. Augustine grass with a hand push mower. He finished the job by meticulously, laboriously, edging with a sharpened shovel. Next, he washed and waxed the car, by hand. That done, he made repairs to our house or worked on an ongoing project, like building a brick barbecue pit. He always whistled as he worked, happy to be outside in the sun and fresh air. He claimed it was detoxifying to work up a sweat. I followed him around like a pesky puppy asking questions he always had time to answer. He taught me how to soap a screw so it would slip into dense wood like it was butter. He taught me how to drive a nail, straight and true. There is a tall Texas pine tree in the back yard of my old childhood home forever fortified with pounds of ten penny nails.

When he had completed his tasks, he took a shower, made himself a Tom Collins hi-ball and sat down to enjoy a late afternoon baseball game on TV. His pleasure and sense of self-satisfaction was palpable. Sometimes, at our begging, he would forego the game and take us to Stewart beach, an hour away in Galveston, for a romp in the salty Gulf breakers. Returning home, after dark, sand wedged between our toes and plastered miserably in our swimsuits, we'd all fall out of the car in a mad competitive dash for the one bathroom, leaving him behind to clean up. I have no memories of him complaining about anything, except maybe never being able to find his nails and screws.

He wasn't an overtly religious man, but he taught me the Lord's Prayer. He wasn't an educated man, but he loved numbers and he insisted that I learn my multiplication tables by heart, and practiced with me after dinner every night until I knew them upside down and backwards. It was his gentle patience and ability to communicate with me within the framework of my learning zone, that made it possible for me to finally understand the complex mysteries of fractions. This was a teaching skill my college-educated fourth grade teacher did not own. Until recently, I have never thought of these memories in the context of time expended. But now I wonder, when did he have time to do all these things?

There is a lot of discussion, nowadays, about good parenting and what skills, instinctual or acquired, define a good parent. The emphasis primarily centering on time spent with children. Mothers, typically, have always understood the importance of spending time with children and have filled that need naturally. But now modern attitude requires fathers to participate more in the daily care and nurturing of their offspring in an advancing egalitarian effort to "include dad" in the raising of kids. This is good, I agree. Diapering and feeding and bathing does foster a certain amount of bonding. But what about the fundamental significance of good influence? What about the quiet strength and integrity fathers could impart to their children by simply being solid role models? And what makes a good role model? Is it honesty? Is it a strong work ethic? Is it a visible faith in God? All of the above? Yes. But also, I believe it is a genuine interest in, and willingness to meet, the needs of his child, over and above his own needs, beyond his own agendas, physically, emotionally and spiritually.

If I had to declare who had been my primary care giver, I would have to say it was my mother. If parenting hours determine this and could be charted, I'm sure her time invested in me far exceeded that of my dad's. However, there is no denying the dynamic influences of my father are forever entrenched in me. You see, ultimately, it wasn't how much time he had to spend but how he spent it that molded me. And even more importantly, it wasn't as much about time spent, as it was his forthright example that forged me. Frankly, I doubt he ever diapered me. I don't recall him doing any maintenance on me at all, not even kissing a boo-boo. But by virtue of his being a selfless, caring man, willing to listen and share, he was a good... no...he was a great father.

How could he have been more than that?

Confession

*L*ike most creative people I have a bizarre resume. In fact, for most respectable, definable positions of employment, I'm largely unemployable. In my lifelong quest to sample everything, I've managed to experience myself right out of the conventional job market. I've been thinking about this lately, because every New Year I do a self-evaluation to see where I've been and where I'm going. I dug deeply this time and I have a few confessions.

First, and foremost, I can't sell - anything. When I had a small art and gift shop, my customers had to convince me to take their money. I have even been known to talk a shopper out of something, if I thought it wasn't right for her. Could be why I don't have the shop any more. This character flaw goes back, way back, to my Girl Scout cookie selling days. I remember knocking, with trepidation, on the door, holding up my box of cookies and telling my neighbor, " I know you probably won't want to pay fifty cents for these cookies, it's a lot, okay, thanks anyway." A classic candidate for Dale Carnegie, eh?

Secondly, my creativity will never be motivated by profit. This one is a hard pill to swallow when you live with an accomplished businessman who believes every action and reaction should have a dollar value.

Last, but not least, I am an inveterate homemaker (which is the accepted politically correct term for housewife.) There, I said it. During the dynamic sixties and seventies women were encouraged to find themselves through careers so, I dabbled at it, after my youngest started high school, but I never really found my place in the corporate world. It is possible I went back to work just so I could say I was a-this or a-that instead because, like so many others, when filling out applications, I have experienced the degradation and humiliation of the title "housewife".

In recent years, even though there has been a shift in society's collective attitude about women who don't work outside the home, the negative

I Was Just Thinking

images still persist. I have to tell you I really hate the term "stay-at-home-mom". I remember one fine spring day, the year before I opened my shop, I took my grandchildren to a local park. Two young women sat chatting as they watched their kids climb and play. I struck up a conversation with one of them and, as usual, the issue of "what do you do" reared its ugly head. In this setting, I figured I was safe saying I was a professional craft designer and worked out of my home. She responded with that old familiar look of doubt and the unspoken question, "professional what?" She told me the other woman had a home based computer business and then began to hesitate, groping for the words to explain what she did, finally admitting, "I don't do anything". Then she quickly added, "I'm just a mom." My mouth dropped open. Now, normally, I'm not especially outspoken to strangers, but this climbed all over me. I replied to her, "There is no more important job, and never let anyone tell you otherwise." Unfortunately, I could see in her face, my words, alone, would never be enough to elevate her self-image. What a shame.

So, here it is, my confession for the New Year. Simply put, I am a stay at home wife, mother, and grandmother. And even now that I have a home based business and it is easier to tell someone what I do, I am so strongly identified with what I have been for so long, I often forget to mention the writing, design work, and publishing and refer to myself proudly as a homemaker. The emphasis is on *proudly*.

Having said that, I might as well confess that I am to my core a housewife who loves folding clothes, sorting and stacking them into neat, sweet smelling piles. I am deeply satisfied by the serene inner peace of a freshly cleaned house. What is better than the comforting aroma of something tasty and nourishing, floating from the kitchen, made by me, as my husband drags in the door after doing battle with the beast of commerce all day? And contrary to the beleaguered image of housewifery, I am fully able to find creative and productive ways to use my intelligence.

Most of all, I love sitting with a cup of coffee, as the day begins, spending quiet time with the Lord instead of ensnarled in traffic. And, ultimately, I love being able to use all of my creativity doing what I do, instead of just the part a boss or job needs. I am truly grateful I am allowed to be what I am. I know there are those who would gladly take my place. To never take this for granted is my New Year's resolution.

Swinging

I built a swing for my grandchildren...and me. I designed it to rise nine feet above the ground so the arc of the chains would be wide and once in full swing, you'd feel akin to airborne. The kids love it and so do I. Sometimes, in the early mornings, after watering my flowers, I settle into the sling-seat (unfortunately a somewhat snug fit) and push off. It takes stomach muscles for this, muscles I don't really call on much anymore. Awakened, these muscles complain a little and fight back with a tingling sensation. It makes me laugh. There I am, a grandmother hooting and howling, swinging high as possible alone in my back yard. The neighbors must wonder.

But here's the truth, I don't really care what they think; I swing because I have always loved to swing and it keeps me thinking young thoughts, if that's crazy, so be it. When I was six, my parents installed in our yard a tall park-type set with big wooden seats because I was sad about my older sister marrying and leaving home. For the next six years, I spent long, happy hours in that spot. I entertained myself, singing and inventing stories and generally pretending away many a warm Texas afternoon. But most of all, I talked to God there. I guess you could call it prayer, I mostly thought of it as personal conversations. I also studied the clouds as I pumped and pumped, forever striving for record height, maybe even flight. Clouds fascinated me. I promised God that if He would only allow me one hour in the clouds, soaring, I would never tell anyone. I wanted to be in the clouds; at age six, swinging seemed to be my closest option.

Recently, returning home from vacation, I leaned over Ron, who always prefers the window seat, to watch our descent into Hartsfield Airport. Massive white sculptures moved steadily past us, some in the distance, some so close the wings sliced through, disturbing and rearranging them. We were definitely in the clouds, but the feeling was better described that we were among them. I've done this before, many times, in fact. But

I Was Just Thinking

suddenly, this time, I remembered my childhood prayers about flying in the clouds. Drum roll, please, or was it thunder? I smiled at God's great sense of humor and Ron, who is accustomed to me by now, just smiled back without bothering to ask what was so funny. I know God was smiling too, because after all these years, and flights in the clouds, I finally got it.

You see, I know He always answers prayers and I've learned, at last, that rarely does He answer as we expect or in the time frame we think we require. For me it is enough to know that regardless of our puny, narrow, human point-of-view, not to mention impatience, the answer will be timely and precisely right for us even if the answer is no, or not now. The problem is we can't see the big picture from where we are standing.

I guess I'm breaking my original promise by revealing this but I don't think He minds in this case. Deep in thought while swinging, of course, it dawned on me that forty-five years ago He knew I'd tell you about this, so you would be comforted and understand.

Wow!

Faith is not the belief that God will do what you want. It is the belief that God will do what is right.

—Max Lucado

Writing

So, you say you want to be a writer?

For years I played the game strictly according to the rules. I studied the marketplace; the annual Writer's Digest was my Bible. I subscribed to and read magazines that published fiction. I took several courses, both by mail and as extra curricular night classes in a local college. I bought books on writing and read everything I could get my hands on that had anything whatsoever to do with the writing life. I hunted down and devoured Writers On Writing books, reading over and over the ones that spoke of the wolf growling at the door, the car about to be repossessed and then gloriously, in the eleventh hour, the saving acceptance and check in the mail. I loved those.

I edited, pruned and polished everything before I dropped it into the mailbox, all punctuation, grammar, page numbers in the right places, number of lines per page, number of lines from the top to the title, being absolutely sure I had meticulously followed all instructions for submitting a manuscript. I jumped through all the hoops and then some. I even sympathized with editors who are overworked and under appreciated because I know several personally. I kept a log of submissions and rejections, framing the rejections that had nice handwritten comments on them, however brief.

I tried everything I knew to do to break through the barriers. And then one day, walking back from the mailbox, rejection slip in hand from something I had submitted four months prior, I experienced an epiphany. I did a little math in my head and concluded I wasn't getting any younger. I needed to admit, once again, and finally, that I have never been in tune, in step or in time. Never. Serious self-evaluation followed. What I had to face, square on, was that I had become a puppet of the system instead of a budding writer. Not that I don't agree that there has to be rules, but what had happened to me was more about losing whatever genuine creativity I began with in the struggle to be what it appeared everyone wanted from me. Summed up I had completely compromised my true voice, trying to force it to fit and I was not very good at it. One sale in three years was more than likely a fluke rather than an indication I was on my way to becoming a recognized name in print.

Furthermore, and worst of all, I found that I could no longer read for pleasure. Every word and phrase I read, I measured and evaluated, desperately searching for THE FORMULA. There had to be one, I thought. All these published pieces surely had a commonality that I could ferret out and use to advantage. I had already figured out that editors are humans with their own issues and likes and dislikes and guidelines and these also had to be factored in. So many things to consider. Toss in the enormous task of monitoring everything in print to see if a particular publication had already used a similar theme in the past twelve months, one has to become a bit desperate if not hysterical. Unfortunately, desperation and hysteria rarely get you anywhere. Instead of developing ways to eloquently express what was waiting to come out of me, I was filling up my precious time trying to mimic something proven, hoping it would be more marketable than what I really was and certainly instead of risking forcing open new doors.

Standing just in the shadows watching this process was a sinister reality. Though I fully knew it was there, it took me years to muster the courage to call it into the light. Simply put, I didn't have what anyone wanted and there was no way I would be able to fake it even if I did happen upon the illusive formula. And though formulas work, of course, they never refill the deep well from where refreshing creativity springs, anyway. When I began the quest to become a published writer what I had wanted most, even more than fame and fortune, was to find out if, indeed, I had something worthwhile to contribute. In spite of the lack of acceptance, I held tight to the belief that I did and one day I would find a way to get it out.

When I came to this fork in the road I didn't stop writing, I just stopped submitting. It took awhile but eventually, I was able to read again for the shear joy of it. And with perseverance, I found satisfying places to use my writing and peculiar voice. The feedback from the readers of my column, who take the time to email me from all over the world and tell me they enjoy and relate to my writing, is enough to keep me writing it. My puppet stories give me an outlet for my fiction. And though I couldn't possibly have predicted what my life altering decision to change direction would do for my writing, I knew that I couldn't continue on the path I was stumbling down and grow as a writer.

The unexpected result was that, over time, my writing improved dramatically. Staying true to the discipline of writing every day, striving to continue to mature and develop coupled with the freedom to write without formulaic constrictions slowly strengthened my skills and ultimately my confidence. What I have evolved into is a writer who is confident that I can and will continue to develop and grow. I believe in my voice and style now, fragmented sentences and all, and I'm not ashamed to admit it feels quite good. Several years ago, I even felt so secure I took a chance and submitted short stories to an anthology for Georgia writers and had three out of four accepted in two volumes. And the competition was serious, I'm proud to say.

You know, it's easy to conclude, "ah, classic story, she wasn't tough enough for the business," but I think I'm plenty tough because it takes a certain courage and strength of conviction to acknowledge that you do not fit into the mainstream and move on resolutely to find another venue for your skills.

As I look back a recurring pattern seems to be emerging.

Write something to suit yourself and many people will like it; write something to suit everybody and scarcely anyone will care for it.

-Jesse Stuart

Magic Carpet Quilt

*W*hat is the point of recording history? For one thing, so we won't forget. Forgetting is so easy to do. And, oddly enough, when we make room for history in our lives somehow we are granted a clarion blueprint for the future. We often take this for granted. I'm ashamed to say I understood this better when I was less smart.

When I was a child, I would take my mom's "friendship" quilt, by that time already an antique, to a corner of the yard and spread it out in the lush St. Augustine in that transitional moment when late afternoon gently retires to early evening. The thick blades of grass would poke up and make the quilt look as though it were afloat, suspended over the earth by a zillion green spikes. The worn, limp fabric was cool and soft. Lying on my belly, in the fading light, I could examine, up close and personal, the tiny stitches and each embroidered signature; names of women lost to history, names from the turn of the century, strange and antique to a child of the fifties - Irma, Bernice, Lida, Effie, Maude, Ada, Erlene. Only with deep concentration, could I imagine the faces that went with these names.

As the day slipped away, so imperceptibly it almost seemed as though I had imagined it, I tried to conjure up the lives of the ladies who once, long ago, had lovingly recorded their names, for posterity, with floss and needle on what had become my magic carpet. What were they like? How did they live? Did they dream of distant, exotic places as I did? When they were children, did they pretend they were royalty or artists or ballerinas? When they grew up, did they realize their dreams? Was this quilt all there was left of these people? Did they make a difference by being alive?

I wanted to tell them that I, at least, gave thought to their existence.

I would lie there thinking and listening for the emerging hollow night noises. A dog barking. A screen door slamming. Bugs bugging. Twilight is a magic little space in time; the air denser. Any noise seems muted and remote. It is a place where things have to slow down, listen and be thoughtful; the perfect time for serious ten year old reflections on the human condition.

Once the light was completely spent, I'd roll over to my back and wait for the first star to appear. It wasn't something that just happened, first I had to imagine it; to focus on a place where I thought one would eventually be. And when the pinpoint of light suddenly became visible, it was as though it had always been there. And, of course, it had. Cold fact often spoils magic and therefore was not relevant nor welcome in my revere. I never considered, however, that it would be possible to count the stars. For one thing, I've always had the highest esteem for God's universe and the infinity involved. You simply can't count infinity. I surely wanted to go there, though. I wanted in the worst way to be able to take flight and become one with the heavens. To travel unencumbered around the planets. To see the vastness. To understand. I wanted to embrace the universe, to reassure it and thereby be reassured. I delighted in knowing that the women who had made the quilt had looked upon the exact same stars and planets and moon. It was something, besides the quilt, I could share with them, bridging the decades between us. There is comfort in continuity.

I still have that quilt, an inheritance. It is now too fragile to use and hangs, like art, in my guest room; a quaint, slowly decaying reminder of all that is folly about trying to leave behind material markers of our presence on this planet. Ultimately, I believe, the only memorial and testimony to our existence should be the other souls we have nurtured and encouraged to carry on with all that is worthwhile about this life.

When it is time for me to account for myself, I want to be able to say, I took the time to dream and strive for good more often than bad. I taught the ones who came after me to do the same.

Christmas Past

I took a much needed break and sat perfectly still with a cup of coffee in the relative quiet of my living room. Christmas 2002 is culminating and the worst of the frenzy is accomplished and I am grateful to reflect on having survived, nearly every task ticked off my long list.

My vision blurred as I studied the lighted Christmas tree, adorned with now ragged ornaments made by the children a lifetime ago. I gave into reverie and allowed my mind to wander through forgotten doors of Christmas past. You know what I realized? The Christmases that stand out the most for me, in recollection, were the hardest ones. The ones spent separated from family. The ones when I had no money to buy gifts. The ones when I wasn't sure where I'd be and what would happen to me in the New Year.

I especially recall the year my mom, dad, and I moved to Akron, Ohio from Cincinnati because my dad had been transferred. Mother and I drove up in a blinding snowstorm a few weeks after Dad was settled. On December 23rd I decided, regardless of the late hour, we needed a tree. Times were especially tough that year, money scarce to non-existent, circumstances tentative, but I struck out in the family fifty-nine Ford Fairlane determined to find a tree, hopefully a cheap one. At dusk, I found a tree lot still open with a big sign out front that said "All Trees, $2.00". I pulled in and picking the best of what remained, I gleefully hauled it back to our new residence. Frankly, I don't remember what it was decorated with, but I vividly recall it smelled just like Christmas. The next day, on Christmas Eve, my mom gave me $10 to go buy presents to put under the tree. I spent about three hours in the dime store laboring over the exact best way to spend that fin. On Christmas morning, as meager as our celebration was, we were grateful for a roof over our heads and food to eat.

I kept thinking, and this too shall pass.

Funny how your mind locks into these times, the details fresh and poignant and all the good ones just sort of blend together into a vague collective warm feeling with no particular memory to bring forward to peruse. I can also fast forward these to a number of difficult Christmases while raising my kids and a couple of really bad ones that, even so, had something redeeming to count. Maybe it's just me, and the way I ride the waves as they come, but it seems to me, that my worst experiences have always been the defining moments of the development of my character.

What is true about our lives is that we own nothing except our attitude and control nothing really. But deep inside every moment, good and bad, we have the choice before us to determine what the moment will do to us in the long run. Every day, every challenge puts us at a fork in the road. That's just the way it is. We can grieve and become dysfunctional or we can find something to turn for good out of our misery.

I think the bleak days of our lives afford us the opportunity to test what we are truly made of. Not losing heart or succumbing to despair in the face of trouble sends a message to adversity that you will not only survive the worst of times, but triumph, emerging stronger. If, for some reason, you feel you are slipping, look up and out and do something kind for someone less fortunate than yourself. There will always be those more as well as less fortunate than we. Somehow, we gain perspective when we look out of our own darkness.

And when it looks as though you might not make it, never forget...

And this too shall pass.

Although the world is full of suffering, it is full also of the overcoming of it.
—Helen Keller (1880 - 1968)

Downtime

*F*or several years I was employed as a commercial photo stylist. In fact, it was the job that brought me to Atlanta from Tulsa. The 50,000 square foot studio that housed the photographers, copy editors, graphic artists and stylists, all collaborating on impossible deadlines, was visibly throbbing with intense creative energy. Honestly, it was amazing.

    I was completely overwhelmed in the first few weeks because I had come from a more laid back work environment. Also, I started just as the Christmas catalog crunch had begun to rev up. Nevertheless, I had no choice but to do it. If I didn't understand or hadn't experience in the product styling I was assigned - too bad. Since I didn't want anyone to know, I faked it until I had a grip on it. I asked questions, offhandedly, of course, and observed everyone, making copious mental notes. I've always been pretty good at mimicking. This is a dubious skill that has carried me through many learning curves. Though it was a tense time in my life, by the will of God, I hung on until, eventually, I was able to handle most anything thrown my way from elaborate bed sets to food. While mayhem and chaos fairly describe the hectic phases during this period, there was one saving grace. Downtime.

    When the last shot of the last seasonal catalog lay approved on the light box, the whole building heaved with one huge sigh of relief. Everyone knew there would be close to two weeks before the next big drive would hit. Suddenly, the previously tumultuous studio was dark and cavernous. All the freelance shooters and stylists, temporarily hired on to help with the work load, were gone. In the morning, there was time to have a cup of coffee in the break room and peruse several months worth of Advertising Age and Photo District News that had stacked up unopened. Without much need for assigning, everyone voluntarily chose menial clean up tasks. The photographers straightened their sets, repaired and replaced equipment and cleaned and rolled their extension cords into neat coils.

The stylists purged and sorted the prop room and styling kitchen and took time to scan decorator and design magazines, pulling swipes for their personal style reference binders. The music on the PA was more mellow and restful. It was a time for recharging. Most artists understand this process instinctively, but it is a dynamic that should apply to anyone because each of us needs periodic downtime whether we admit it or not.

Because of my work experience, I am in tune with this fundamental human requirement. I know when I need it and am able to recognize the signs instantly - inability to concentrate, lack of patience, wandering thoughts, memory loss, restlessness, bottled up creativity, mild depression. Sleep is really just daily physical downtime; the body takes over here. But there is a more subtle, easy to circumvent, emotional downtime that we, unfortunately, in this high speed society, are programmed to ignore. No amount of sleep will help.

We aren't comfortable unless we are being productive and unfortunately, by our own standards, clean-up doesn't count. The conclusion of every day must be held accountable to some measure of meaningful progress. High blood pressure, heart attacks and strokes are the results of this relentless, mechanical demand on our worthiness. There is no question, bad diet contributes, of course, but, I believe, not allowing the recharging and reversing of our gears is what can kill, if not our bodies, then at least, our spirits and ultimately, our ability to visualize and create. Put simply, we never give ourselves the right to be unscheduled. That is why vacation isn't downtime. Downtime is not about getting away or playing or planned activity. It is more about dulling down to allow for contrast. In this contradictory life, it is a given that everything gains it's significance by contrast. In the studio, by the end of downtime, we were so bored, our creative juices were foaming and literally spilling out, ready and eager for the next challenge. The last few days before work resumed, we were like race horses held back at the gates, muscles twitching, ready to run hard and fast once again.

Before I left, a communications company bought the studio. They were a management group, essentially bean counters, who did not recognize the basic concept of downtime. As far as they were concerned, people who weren't churning out photos weren't earning their salaries and thus not enlarging the bottom line. My first internal warning bell began clanging when the order came down to make everyone fill out hourly time cards that recorded daily activity in six minute intervals in military time. I didn't stay much longer after that, because it got worse, real fast. In a matter of months, upon entering the building, a wall of stress and tension met you like a negative electric field.

You see, the powers in charge ignored the human element, thereby leaving out the most valuable contribution to productivity and finally good product - enthusiasm for the work - which, if they had cared to research, only comes from the cyclic recharging of the batteries before burnout occurs. If you haven't stopped to recognize this phenomenon of the human spirit, you probably aren't being good to yourself. How can you be your best for anything or for anyone, if you can't give yourself the gift of downtime?

You know you need it, so, go ahead. I give you permission.

Every now and then go away, have a little relaxation, for when you come back to your work your judgment will be surer. Go some distance away because then the work appears smaller and more of it can be taken in at a glance and a lack of harmony and proportion is more readily seen.

—Leonardo Da Vinci

Free Will

*H*ave you ever been in a tight situation and made a promise to do or be something else if only the hard circumstances would ease and the outcome turn out in your favor? Did you follow through when all was said and done? In other words, did you keep your promise?

Interesting thing about promises is that they are almost always toward a higher good, aren't they? I mean, think about it. A child who promises his parent that he will behave or clean his room or stop pestering his little sister is actually promising to rise to an already assumed expectation of that which he knows he should be doing anyway. A kid never promises to be a liar or a thief or a bully, does he?

So, cutting to the chase, we know right from wrong instinctively, even from a very young age. We know what God expects of us, if we are willing to admit it. So it isn't much of a stretch to promise that we will conduct ourselves appropriately when our finger is caught in a ringer. We also know when to be sneaky and to lie to protect ourselves from a chastisement that we fully understand would result from being caught. Just like kids.

We are children who already know what their parent wants from them. What we don't understand is that, like a good parent, God not only wants what is best for us and He wants us to trust that He knows what that might be, He also wants us to grow up spiritually with grace so that we will easily recognize and make the good choices that are in our own best interest. Thus He wants us to truly want what He wants, not merely identify what it is. This is a subtle distinction to grasp, but important, nonetheless.

However, wanting what He wants always means giving up certain things, and that might be the crux of our obstinacy. First of all it requires forfeiting our right to ourselves, and tuning in to what we know to be true about the higher good. Secondly it means leaning on Him without reservation and accepting that what we had planned might not have been the direction He wanted us to take and then willingly leaving it behind without lingering doubt. Did He not admonish Lot and his family to not look back? Remember what happened to his wife when she just had to take one last sentimental look?

What is asked of us is abandonment of our free will in exchange for His will. Letting go of free will means surrender, to be sure, but it is also blind acceptance and faith in the supernatural power of God to know, better than we, what path we should be taking. He wants us to not only choose the higher good, He wants us to experience the sheer joy of truly wanting the higher good.

This, then, is the conundrum of free will. God wants us to choose to come to Him, to choose His way, so He gives us opportunities to decide, yes or no. But He wants us to do so willingly, not simply because we don't want to get into trouble. Taking the high road by cowardice may keep our hands clean, but it won't instill in us the nature of God. Goodness in and of itself is only a veneer. Only the deep solid grain of God's genuine goodness dwelling in us can last against the ravages of time and adversity. Desiring this is the only way to get it. Getting it means not looking back to your old ways with sentimentality. It also means practicing. We have to exercise our faith muscle in order for it to grow. We must be ready to listen and obey, without question the small promptings in order to practice listening and obeying the life altering prompts.

But, like children, we still want to have choices. We want to be the captains of our destiny. And, like children, when we make our bad choices we still want our loving parent to come to our rescue. So, we get in our tight spots and boldly make our promises to be and do what we knew we should have been and done in the first place.

I'm so grateful that He is patient and has all the time in the universe but I am painfully aware that we are the ones who run out of time.

On Turning Fifty

As I opened bottles and little bubble packs, carefully lining up my morning supplements on the counter - my vitamin, my hormone pill, my Ginkoba (for mental acuity), my Ginseng (for sagging energy) and my calcium (for shrinking bones), I had a flashback.

I saw my aging mom and dad, coming for a visit. They brought with them three suitcases - one each for clothing, plus one other - for their medications. I am now ashamed to admit that, at the time, we all sort of made light of this. My parents, each being rich with a keen sense of humor, however, never took offense and perhaps took quiet solace in the knowledge that we would understand ... one day.

They, of course, were right.

It's not that I'm unhealthy. I am, in fact, in good shape for my advanced years and none the worse for the wear and tear that active living has inflicted on my body. But I've been forced to face there is no escaping the reality of getting older. Parts do wear out. Gravity is a two-edged sword; it keeps us from falling off the earth but in the process then continues to pull all firm things southward. I'm not fighting it, exactly. Let's just say, I'm negotiating.

Now, I didn't mind so much the gray hair suddenly appearing; there are simple ways to deal with this. And I'm proud to say I haven't complained too loudly about all those new subtle aches and pains or allowed the threat of them to stop me from diving into any physical thing I have wanted to do. I will admit I wasn't happy about the obnoxious loss of my good vision, on or about my fortieth birthday. Although, even this can be considered a blessing when you are forced to face your decline in the mirror everyday. Only your closest friends and family members (or dolts of exceptionally bad breeding) would be boorish enough to bring to your attention the two inch wild hair on your chin. (The whole chin hair thing is another story anyway.)

I Was Just Thinking

Being fair, I can't blame aging for my bilateral foot surgery. No one tied me up when I was young and made me wear those four-inch, spike-heeled, pointy-toed torture chambers while my poor feet were still developing. With the grace of a mature adult, I accept full responsibility for this one.

Memory loss. This I resent. It's so unfair. I have spent fifty years gathering, processing and filing information to be accessed and used at will. How I hate those synapse misfires. Frustration doesn't fully describe the helplessness of not being able to call up a simple, ordinary word - or remember the name of the actress who played Emma Peale on "The Avengers". Not that I would ever need this trivia, but we're talking the principle of the thing here. This is just tacky. I view this as hitting below the belt and although I realize that others, like myself, labeled "Boomers", are experiencing the same phenomenon, this doesn't give me much comfort when I'm trying to impress someone with my ...uh...you know... what is that word?... means important...oh yeah, *wisdom* and can't recall the adjective, *valuable*.

Well, what are you gonna do? Laugh like my parents did, I suppose... and get a big suitcase for all your pills.

Bummer.

To the outside world we all grow old. But not to brothers and sisters. We know each other as we always were. We know each other's hearts. We share private family jokes. We remember family feuds and secrets, family griefs and joys. We live outside the touch of time.

-Clara Ortega

Impatiens

Sometime in mid-May, every year, I am driven by the overwhelming urge to get all my spring/summer planting done post haste so that my tender blooming annuals will have time to flourish and mature by the first of July. I assume I have an internal governor that controls this, thus assuring I will be rewarded for as much summer as possible with the blooming fruits of my back-breaking labors. This year was different though.

Oh, I did indeed scurry to get my favorites in the pots on my deck (having finally learned the local deer cannot destroy them there.) I did a cursory pruning of the other beds hoping for new growth on the perennials I have planted in previous years. But in anticipation of my summer being hectic, realizing that I would be missing in action for much of June, I left some pots unplanted fearing they might not get watered and thus die anyway. I even stuck one of them, dry dirt and all, behind some larger pots, hiding its ugly emptiness from view.

May rolled over into June and June morphed into July. One thing after another kept me away from my yard and deck pots. They didn't seem to mind being left to their own natural devices and what with the exceptional amount of rain we have had this year, my Begonias, Coleus, Amethyst Flowers, Stella d'Oros, Pincushions, Dusty Millers and other assorted plantings, whose names I do not know, happily filled out and blossomed even in my absence.

By early August, things having calmed down, I occasionally paused, in a spare moment, to stare out the side door, with deep pang of regret, at the pot under our bedroom window that still sat barren and forlorn. I recalled fondly the previous years and the cascading bright pink blooms that had usually taken over the spot by that time. I couldn't bring myself to go to the trouble to do a late planting. "Oh well, next year," I consoled myself.

And then, by mid-August, I noticed tiny green sprouts in that pot. I thought, "Well, what do you know, last year's Impatiens are trying to come back." I had no real hope for any spectacular rebirth before summer's end so I let them be. A week later I discovered the pot was miraculously blooming from one end to the other. Furthermore, the pot of dead soil that I had hidden was blooming as well and I gleefully dragged it out in front. No doubt I will be enjoying these bouquets at least until Thanksgiving – two full months in the distance. Amazing!

There is a lesson here, I'm sure of it. The obvious seems to conclude that I am too boxed in to fixed expectations and I really should lighten up. I live my life by the clock, list and calendar, scurrying around making sure everything is done according to a schedule. This has to be done by that time and that has to be done by this time or...what? In my efficient life-processing I fear I am missing out on some really good serendipidous joy.

Or what?

I can't answer that. But like I said, there's a lesson here for me if not all of us.

Maybe you can figure it out.

> There is no royal road to anything, one thing at a time, all things in succession. That which grows fast, withers as rapidly. That which grows slowly, endures.
>
> —Josiah Gilbert Holland

Picture Book Grandmother

Something has gone awry. This realization has me stymied. First of all, I see clearly that I am not the grandmother that I had long envisioned I would be; apparently, I'm not going to be, ever. Furthermore, I'm hacked to admit this and secondly, topping off this annoyance, summer, I find, is way shorter than it used to be.

Although I can claim to be a fairly credible grandparent, full of fun things to do with diminutive people, ages twenty months to eleven years, still, I am not that perfect granny portrayed in all the picture books. You know the one. She covers her limber physic with a huge flowing linen shirt, her hair is silk, streaked with white and wound up into an off-centered knot, loose tendrils falling out at will. Think Katherine Hepburn. She often wears a big straw hat and smudges of oil paint permanently reside on the side of her nose or cheek. She paints wonderfully, by the way, great sweeping panoramas of the white sandy dunes fringed with sea oats and wispy clouds that kiss the horizon behind the swelling blue-green ocean that is her back yard.

Picture book grandmothers almost always live at the ocean, it turns out, where children can run barefoot in the surf all morning, collecting seashells, chasing hermit crabs and being chased in turn by squealing sea gulls. Then, after lunch, they get a painting lesson or listen with wide-eyed surprise to the ocean-like sounds in a big pink conch shell. They write poems and shell peas on the front porch. Together, child and wizened senior, they weed the garden and pick armloads of flowers as the long, lazy summer inches its way into midyear like a snail on the porch step. Vacation time with grandmother is always memory making... in picture books. More importantly, time spent with this kind of grandmother stands still.

I'm sitting here looking at my garden after granddaughter and I finish reading a couple of library books in the arbor swing. This is when it hits me. The weeds are so tall I hadn't even noticed that my nemesis, the resident neighborhood deer, has chewed my salmon colored begonia to the nub. My garden, the one I permanently damaged my back digging and planting in the spring, is now a wasteland of lanky green wild grasses and bloomless, half eaten perennials. When granddaughter gets up and wanders off to find more interesting things to do than sit with me, I suddenly understand that I'm losing ground in the most subtle of ways.

I am also losing time, I observe.

With more life behind me than in front of me, I am rapidly running out of wiggle room. I don't have the luxury to dawdle and piddle around trying to decide what I want to be later, where I want to end up, whom I want to evolve into. Furthermore, I am truly annoyed to admit that my body is no longer as young as my mind and complains more loudly and often than it used to. My body is no longer so forgiving of my lifting eight foot four by four landscaping timbers anymore. My knees are less than happy about doing the kneeling required in gardening, as well. My back, the biggest whiner of all my parts, rebels continuously; though lifting eight foot four by fours might contribute to this, I concede.

My shortcomings suddenly rush in on me from all sides. It hackles me to note that not only is my hair not long, I am a mediocre painter, at best. And, insult heaped on injury, though I live on a nice lake where grandchildren can plunge into deep water from the top of the dock, I do not live at the ocean in a quaint cottage with a front porch.

Could I be more of a disappointment?

I know that if my grandchildren were polled they would likely vote me in as Grandmother of the Year, I'm that confident in my grandmothering skills. But still there remain those empty credentials in my grandmother resume that will likely never be completed. It is a bittersweet epiphany.

More than anything, this getting older thing is a major nuisance because the clock appears to be ticking faster. Summer no longer drifts endlessly like puffy clouds on a warm breeze. The pages on the calendar are flipping furiously as though caught in a gale force wind. July Fourth, which used to be the real start of summer, now flashes by and burns out instantly like a burst of fireworks. Once this date whizzes past, all further summering must be crammed, it seems, into a few short weeks. How absurd is that?

I conclude it boils down to this: I hate being told, "you can't" or "you won't" and I loathe to admit that I very likely will not accomplish all those goals I had set for myself because it is an inexplicable phenomenon of life that time speeds up, as you age, like the last grains of sand in the hourglass. The analogy ends there, though, because you don't get to turn it over and start again. When the sand is gone, it's gone. I can't stop it from flowing and I don't really know how to make peace with this. Maybe I should stop reading those "Grandmother and I" picture books.

Maybe I should write one.

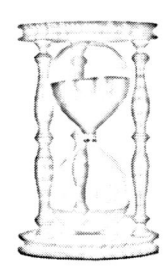

Everyone knows on any given day that there are energies slumbering in him which the incitements of that day do not call fourth. ... Compared with what we ought to be, we are only half awake. Our fires are damped, our drafts are checked. We are making use of only a small part of our possible mental and physical resources. ... Stating the thing broadly, the human individual thus lives far within his limits he possesses powers of various sorts he habitually fails to use.

—William James

Curiosity

*N*ovelist, Lawrence Naumoff, who teaches creative writing classes in a university, is quoted as saying he sees a bad trend in his students. They have no curiosity, no interest in learning for the sake of learning. They attend his class, never find out his name, and get what they have to in order to get a grade. This is both sad and scary to me because it reveals a major societal downturn. Not that I am surprised, I've been watching this slow slide for decades. The last time I brought it up was in a debate in my Advanced English class in 1964 and met with such distain, I've kept it to myself ever since. I guess it is safe to speak about this now since others are beginning to see the light.

It is a given that collected general knowledge is the engine of problem solving; problem solving is the foundation of positive growth. If we cannot figure out how to make do with what we have and what we know, then we end up like many of the hurricane Katrina evacuees, not all of which allowed themselves to be ignored by inept government. Helplessness is not a sign of positive growth in the human condition. If we are moving forward in the wrong direction, we might as well be moving backwards.

Some might argue against this but I believe modern technology is at the root of this trend and is, at the same time, both friend and curse to civilization. Because of constant and ever changing technology, there is so much that is new to learn, all things old must be kicked to the curb. This includes most of the greatest most inspirational and elevating elements and processes of civilized society and human achievement acquired at enormous cost. But who cares anymore? The scramble to know about the *latest* thing seems to have overtaken the need to spend time learning what we have gained from the past. Unfortunately, all that is new to learn is not always worth learning but we are coaxed to believe if we are to survive in a high tech world, we must keep up so we spend our time learning it anyway. We think we are being productive because we now have things that save us time, and we tell ourselves that we are so smart for all we know even as we grow dumber and dumber. We don't have to commit anything to memory anymore because some soulless device keeps all the data for us. But regardless of how many conveniences we have at our fingertips, time is one thing that cannot be saved. It moves on. To compensate we cut back minutes in one activity only to add on minutes to another. In the end, we find we are hustling faster, sleeping less and worrying more…and ultimately, for all our trouble, knowing less and less. And when the lights go out or the batteries die, all our data is useless to us. We stand there, ignorant as babes.

Today there is so much information to assimilate, it all must be compartmentalized, divided and doled out in specialized increments. This narrowing down of focus is so pervasive in our culture now, which effects how and what people choose to learn, it spans all industries and professions. The practice of medicine is a prime example of specialization and reduction of broad knowledge. There is no such thing as a liberal education any more, which means there is a huge loss of general curiosity about many and assorted things. Who has time to be curious about anything that does not pertain to the moment at hand?

Unfortunately, what is forgotten about the benefits of knowing a little about a lot and grasping the bigger picture of how all things work together, is that life, regardless of all its new innovations, continues to be made of many experiences. Some of these are thrown at us suddenly and unexpectedly. Problem solving is born of multiple opportunities of having been able to apply liberal knowledge. If we lose our ability to solve problems that we have never been faced with before simply because we have no baseline of common knowledge to draw from, we become completely vulnerable to disaster.

This then is the point.

When we lose our natural curiosity and love of learning for the sake of learning, eventually we forget how to learn deeply and, more importantly, how to discern what is significant to our ability to survive independently. It is a very bad sign, albeit true, that the more basic problem solving skills we lose because we are trusting in someone or something else to be responsible for our survival, the less chance we have to survive. But it is ever so, and a rule of the natural world, that no one is as interested in

I Was Just Thinking

an individual's wellbeing than the individual him/herself. Does it make sense then to ignore the basic answer of doing what is in our own best interest and learning how to learn, to be curious and garner information that can not only improve us as humans but society as a whole?

B.F. Skinner said: "Education is what survives when what has been learned has been forgotten" And ... "The real problem is not whether machines think but whether men do."

So, who is B.F. Skinner?

I have no idea, but I bet I will go find out.

Cultivate your garden... Do not depend upon teachers to educate you ... follow your own bent, pursue your curiosity bravely, express yourself, make your own harmony... In the end, education, like happiness, is individual, and must come to us from life and from ourselves. There is no way; each pilgrim must make his own path. "Happiness," said Chamfort, "is not easily won; it is hard to find it in ourselves, and impossible to find it elsewhere."

-Will Durant

Delusions

She's standing ahead of me. This is painfully symbolic. We are both in line waiting for our turn to vote. Judging by the way we are not moving, it appears we have at least a good wait ahead of us. I'm glad, actually, because I've needed to study her, up close, for sometime now. I've never seen her before so I don't know her personally, of course, but I feel I know her very well.

She is the grown up representation of all the girls I wanted to be. She is the one who somehow garnered all the good sense when I was off on an artistic tangent. She was the one who had social skills and a strong game plan for her future, from the tender age of six, while I was swept up in daydreams of being a ballerina or actress or famous painter. In high school she was a cheerleader and member of the elite group while I was immersed in an alternate universe with the right-brained bohemian thespians. She wore the perfect clothes, had the perfect hairstyle, polished Bass Weejun loafers covered her perfectly arched feet. Her graceful hands tipped with freshly manicured nails are, even now, flawless as ever. Adding insult to injury, her polished charm is not tainted with the slightest hint of arrogance.

How annoying is that?

I recognized her immediately because she exudes grace that she was most certainly born with. How can you fault someone who was born with it? Time has been most kind to her. She is still a slender, ideal five foot four. Her starched striped oxford shirt is neatly tucked into pressed khakis. I notice she has updated the loafers though. She is a balanced combination between classic good taste and new era fashion.

Actually the first thing that draws my attention is her hair. She's still sporting that amazing ageless pageboy. Well, of course she is. It works for her, which is her modus operandi and it's predictably reasonable. It's not the choppy spiky modern cut, nor is it grandma helmet head. I would expect nothing less of her to be able to maintain a style that is exactly right at all times, through all decades. I'd really love to ask her where in the world she has found someone who can still cut hair like that but I'm no less intimidated by her personae now than I was in 1964. I wouldn't know how to initiate a conversation with her today anymore than I could have back then.

When she turns her head, I'm taken aback. I note that the Wrinkle Rank puts her at about five years older than I. You would not guess it from the back view. I am not surprised, however, that she hasn't succumbed to Botox. That would be totally inconsistent with her grounded sensibility. But her smile reveals perfect orthodonically aligned teeth.

With plenty of time to waste, I shift my weight to my other bad knee and dive in whole hog to wonder about the last forty years of her life. It wouldn't be a stretch to assume she attended a good college. Being five years older, I doubt she got involved in the Vietnam war protests, marches and sit-ins of the late sixties, not to say that she and her sorority sisters hadn't had their good causes though. She earned her BA in the appropriate four years and found a proper job. When she married, she had a fairytale wedding and she and her new husband settled into a cozy apartment, diligently saving their money to buy their first home, a modest suburban ranch before starting their family on perfect cue. She quit her job to stay home and raise her children but kept busy volunteering at the school and a variety of other community based organizations including a good church. She was terrific at it too, because, being sensible, she never overbooked herself so that she could give each project her undivided attention until it was completed. She is likely an alumnus and mentor of the local Junior League and she leads a Sunday school class.

She was born and raised to make good choices, after all, and she did, and continues to do so. Even though her children have probably married and divorced at least once each, she and her husband of thirty-five years continue to be the anchor to the family boat. Amidst the raging financial and relationship storms of the current era they stand strong together, unified by the good, middle-of-the-road decisions they have made, working hard, acquiring material goods only after saving for them and compromising their core values only when compromise was the best way to end conflict.

She represents the hero of my hormonal, idealistic, willful youth and she remains the champion of what remains of the prudent, refined, well-balanced woman of a rapidly declining civilized culture. Intelligent but not aggressively so, she is able to form solid opinions that keep her on the straight and narrow path with a comfortable margin on either side. Her well-earned unassuming self-confidence has stood her in a good and unwavering stead.

I am not foolish enough to think she has never had troubles or grief in her life. This fantasy of mine is fed and perpetuated by my own enduring misgivings about my irreversible choices and shortcomings, not an unreasonabe rose-colored glasses view of life. There is no logical rationale for why we cling to certain ideals, however absurd they may be, but we just do. Sometimes we have expectations that are like heavy canvas duffle bags that we drag behind us from childhood into maturity and often all the way to our graves. It is unfortunate that we limit ourselves by these self-designed myths rather than giving ourselves permission to let go of our illusions of what constitutes a perfect life.

I'm grateful for this opportunity to pull this burdensome thing out into the light for a closer scrutiny. While I did give up, some time ago, the notion that I could ever be or become this kind of woman, there are traces that linger, constantly threatening to expose my inadequacies and self-inflicted failures. I also finally gave up longing to be a ballerina or a fine-artist as well, though this was much less difficult given my genuine lack of skills or training in these pursuits. I accept that I am what I am and whatever that is I give it everything I've got however sub-standard it might be. I'll never live up to my own expectations but then, it never occurred to me, until now, that maybe she didn't either. What if she would have enjoyed being more erratic and less sensible? Maybe she would have loved a shot at diving in to the middle with reckless abandon, working her way out to both ends without the burden of sensibility binding her to the best possible approach.

What if this woman, who has always made her hard life choices based on an inherent wisdom, keeping what is in her own best interest as the priority, might also have had regrets about those safe choices? Imagine how it feels, after all these years, to consider that this icon of my lifelong delusions might have thought life would be less ordered but infinitely

I Was Just Thinking

more fulfilling if lived less wisely and more serendipitously. What if she has wanted to be more like my kind all along? Some delusions are infinitely better than others, especially if they make you feel good about yourself.

Maybe I'll go with this new one for a while.

What is opportunity, and when does it knock? It never knocks. You can wait a whole lifetime, listening, hoping, and you will hear no knocking. None at all. You are opportunity, and you must knock on the door leading to your destiny. You prepare yourself to recognize opportunity, to pursue and seize opportunity as you develop the strength of your personality, and build a self-image with which you are able to live / with your self-respect. alive and growing.

—Maxwell Maltz

Saving Summer

The deep center of July used to be the half-way point of summer vacation. Stretching out in front of that marker lay as many lazy, unstructured days as there were drifting behind it in steamy wisps of memory. Sadly this is no longer true. Educators and law-makers have determined that children need to be in school all the time. It's called 45/15 or, in other words, year-round school. The number of days required by Federal law that children must be in school remains at 180 so the issue of how to spread these days out over the year is the root of the year-round-school controversy. Every year a small contingency of die-hard parents speaks out against those who propose 45/15 and just narrowly succeed in pushing it back. Then, every year, those in charge of such things rearrange the calendar to pump in more days off during the academic year, thus stealing from the length of summer vacation anyway. So far, this diabolical plan is working. Summer holiday now begins earlier in May but ends even as July does.

I swear I don't know what they could be thinking but then I have a slightly different definition for education and what makes up a good solid scholastic foundation. Many school districts, now under the gun to prove how good they are, and thus maintain their jobs and Federal funding, grasp desperately at solutions to streamlining the process of filling up kids with information. It is a general concensus that the answer lies in making the time allowed to do it more contiguous. Certainly, kids lose less information if there is less time between lessons. Twelve to thirteen weeks of summer vacation means that teachers often must spend the first six weeks immersed in review of the previous school year. Okay, so what? Anyone over age twenty-five did exactly this their entire school careers, which includes even those esteemed credentialed educators who have now decided children cannot be properly prepared if they squander three months not hitting the books.

Pardon me for asking, but did summers off thwart these folks from getting to where they are?

At the heart of my somewhat skewed perspective, information and more of the same piled higher and deeper doesn't constitute education anyway. Learning how to learn and learning to love learning is what we really should be going for, isn't it? If you look at it from the practical side, all that data in/data out is mostly just practising the skills of learning. The marginally hidden crux of it all isn't so-much-data-so-little-time, it's about appearances and numbers. Unfortunately, the numbers are stacked against all school districts now because the quest to truly educate has been derailed by the mandate to prove that we are educating.

If we sincerely wanted to expose the root of the problem of declining grade averages and waning interest in learning, perhaps we should look instead to lazy parenting, abysmal role models from the entertainment/sports industry and superficial values hammered into our children from movies/television, advertising and the print media. Not even year-round school can begin to overcome these destructive influences. Let us remember that 180 days is still just 180 days. School is not the only place where children can be filled up with information.

Getting down to it, what is it that we are really expecting of our children?

I know I am spitting in the wind. I realize my grandchildren will not have the same life experiences that I had or even that of their parents; that's the way it is. Change is the only constant. I'm certainly not one of those fogies who believes that only the "old" ways are the best. But when the merciless summer sun is retiring late in the hour, cueing the fireflies to begin their fairy dance, I hear the rising call of the cicada and remember when life seemed considerably easier to digest. There was time for everything, even nothing. Perhaps this is just another illusion of mine but one thing is true, historically the most enduring cultures that have survived all earth changes continue to understand and honor the basic human need to rest and have downtime.

Kids can't miss what they've never had, it's true, but it is also true that human psyche is the same now and forever and that is something no amount of education can alter.

If I could, I'd save summer because long vacations are therapeutic if for no other reason they make you desperate to get back into routine. If it were in my power, I'd proclaim that summer vacations would always last long enough for kids to be so bored out of their gourds they'd be more than ready for another nine months of school; so excited for school to start again that they can't sleep the night before. It always worked for me.

Sometimes it's the littlest things that are the most profound.

> *The Universe is one great kindergarten for man. Everything that exists has brought with it its own peculiar lesson. The mountain teaches stability and grandeur; the ocean immensity and change. Forests, lakes, and rivers, clouds and winds, stars and flowers, stupendous glaciers and crystal snowflakes, - every form of animate or inanimate existence, leaves its impress upon the soul of man. Even the bee and ant have brought their little lessons of industry and economy.*
>
> *-Orison Swett Marden*

Gardeners

*S*he planted flowers wherever she lived. My mother loved flowers. She understood them, and they responded to her loving hand and rewarded her with copious, multicolored blooms all spring, summer and fall. Once her annuals were planted, she spent her mornings pruning and pulling off old blooms, humming and singing quietly, lost in the joy of nurturing. She knew exactly where to pinch the bud of a geranium to make it produce a double bloom. Otherwise humble petunias were lush and exotic looking. They spilled over in tumbling cascades, huge ruffled masses of dewy, velvety blossoms, no matter how hot or dry the weather was. And believe me the weather can be most inhospitable to anything but the hardiest vegetation in Houston. Mother's flowers didn't seem to notice.

She also ignored traditional planting schedules and stuffed anything in the ground, anytime. It was a running joke in our household that everyday when my brother returned from school she would be waiting for him with a shovel and a little digging to do. Gardenias, peach trees, wisteria, fig trees, pear trees, sweet gum, maple, roses, zinnias, iris, grapes, you name it, she had it thriving in our yard.

Over the years, she kept up the horticultural ritual she began as a young woman and continued planting even when she didn't own the house or yard, though her back hurt and her knees were enlarged from arthritis. I always thought it was because she needed the color and gentle beauty of growing things to enliven her sometimes mediocre environments. While this was true, it was only partly so. It wasn't until I was well past having reached adulthood that I understood she was simply living her most basic philosophy - leave it better than you found it .

I am reminded of this point of view every time I drive past the housing projects on Hwy 129 entering Gainesville, Georgia from 985. Squeezed in-between identical decaying bricked facades there is a front stoop and walkway lined with growing things, tall sunflowers, leggy tropicals and assorted pots of blooming color. Apparently, someone else adheres to the principle of leaving it better than you found it. I've never seen anyone cultivating this little garden so I have no idea who is keeping it, male or female, but I have an indelible image in my mind of an older lady, knees swollen, humming softly as she digs around in her pots and shores up her heavy-headed sunflowers with bits of salvaged string. I want to meet her and give her a big hug. To me she is a champion, a symbol of everything that is worthwhile about the human spirit. She is an example of an indomitable consciousness and one of a dying breed in our society. Her efforts shine, against immeasurable odds. She is a gardener. I read once that gardeners were earthbound angels, driven somehow to bring something of Heaven here. Perhaps that is what Dorothy Frances Gurney meant when she penned,

> *The kiss of the sun for pardon,*
> *The song of the birds for mirth;*
> *One is nearer to God's Heart in a garden,*
> *Than anywhere else on earth.*

I salute the gardener in Gainesville, whoever he or she may be. We could use more angels.

Simple

July 1998

It is a perfect paddleboat morning. The water is shimmering satin stretched taut between two shores. In this early hour there is nothing disturbing the surface but me, the skate bugs and an occasional fish breaking through. It is painfully beautiful and I am immensely grateful to be here. This has been such a hectic summer, a wedding, a move, a seminar and a dozen other things wedged in-between, I had forgotten how gratifying it is to simply be still.

My ragged thoughts stray to my daughter's friend who lost her way very early in her life. She is now on the road to recovery, having just earned a commendation from AA for being drug free and sober for six months. It has been a long, hard struggle for her to find her way back to normal. She recently told Holly that she was amazed to discover that life was more than just a big party. Obviously, her perspective had been jaded by the artificial things she had filled her life with. By leaving behind her old engulfing habits she had been forced to slow down and experience a more simplistic life. Walking in the park or taking a bike ride, activities she would have ranked as incredibly boring a half year ago have now become fundamentally important to her well-being. She probably doesn't realize that only now is she finding a true balance in her life because she is becoming reacquainted with all of her basic senses, seeing, touching, smelling, and listening. As frail humans we desperately need this balance and yet we constantly do ourselves immeasurable harm by neglecting it. In different ways, but not unlike my daughter's friend, we swallow up our lives with perpetual motion, all consuming activity, believing this will be ultimately satisfying.

It seems to be a nineties mind set to assume we must be productive every single minute of the day. We are consummate list makers. A whole industry has developed around staying organized and efficiently busy, recording and accounting for every second of our waking day in a preprinted daybook. What are we afraid of? Do we think we will be labeled lazy if we cannot account for what we have accomplished every day? And more importantly what exactly are we working so furiously towards? If this incessant movement in pursuit of mindless productivity makes us lose our health and hearts, what then have we really gained? What then have we lost?

Well, FYI, here's a secret I discovered on my paddle boat, sitting perfectly still in the middle of Lake Lanier, it isn't our constantly moving bodies that create efficiency. It is our nurtured minds and spirits. We ride ourselves hard and put ourselves away wet (to use a cowboy's phrase) erroneously thinking we can overcome creative exhaustion with sleep. But it is the simple, often overlooked and sometimes boring moments in our day that can save us from ourselves. If we never allow our bodies to be inert, our subconscious ears must strain to hear the still small voice that directs us in how to live not just effectively, but in a well-balanced state. Our most creative selves spring from deep internal storage banks that can only be replenished with regular infusions of quietude. Unfortunately, it is this restorative tranquillity that we are encouraged to ignore by a productivity oriented society, thus draining and depleting our best, most renewable resource, our ingenuity. The truth that is so hard to hear and understand is that we can never achieve balance by piling on more. We have to let go, empty, remove, delete and say no. Unfortunately, easy to say, harder to do.

It is so trite to say stop and smell the roses but I can't think of a better way to say it. It is a lot easier than saying, "paddle to the center of the lake on a quiet Friday morning and sit very still surrounded by nature and little bugs skittering on the water...."

The ability to simplify means to eliminate the unnecessary so that the necessary may speak.
-Hans Hofmann

Champions

It would be hard not to see the dedication to the task at hand while watching the young medal hopefuls participating in the Winter Olympics. You can see it in their intense faces, their pumped muscles, their strained eyes. They have one focus and that is on being the best. What you can't see is the years of honing that focus, though it isn't hard to imagine. Early morning practices, sacrifices of time and normal youthful activities. Why do they do it? What will the tears, frustrations, aching bodies and tons of money spent reap? Well, for one thing, the promise of fame, fortune and a lifetime of product endorsements. Becoming a champion used to be about setting the standard for the best of the best, but now it seems that it is something else. This disturbs me. I don't know when our culture made the ninety-degree turn, but somewhere along the way, personal best has changed its color from crystal clear to green. And this subtle shift in perspective is pandemic.

Years ago, in the grade school my oldest daughter attended, there was a janitor extraordinaire. Jim was an elderly man, and probably worked to supplement his Social Security. But he did his job with the utmost dignity and confidence. He knew the infrastructure of the old building so well, that if a light flickered anywhere, he mentally could trace the cause to its source. Regardless of which hat he was wearing, be it electrician, carpenter, floor sweeper, toilet unstopper, he applied himself to any task as though the very function of the school depended solely on him. He was the first one there in the morning and the last one leaving at night. He had a quick answer for any question. He knew exactly what supplies were in need of replenishing and he made sure everything was where it should be. But the thing Jim did best was smile. He had a good word to say to everyone and anyone, which was infectious. A few pleasant words exchanged with Jim could brighten the dullest of days. Old Jim had a gift and he used it well and was one of those rarest of human beings who lived his philosophy every day. Jim had what used to be known as a work ethic or sometimes called *pride in the doing*.

In retrospect, I can make safe assumptions that Jim's paycheck did not reflect the long hours given and his sincere dedication to the job. After all, he was a janitor and it is likely he made a janitor's wage. This is the system. And if the system says mopping floors is only worth X, then that's what mopping floors nets. This is why no one ever says "I want to be a janitor when I grow up." But Jim did it. And regardless of the road that lead him to the job, he accepted it with grace and dived into it with style and good spirit. He made it look easy and more importantly he made it look as though it was the best job in the world. To my way of thinking, Jim achieved not only his personal best, he made a faultless contribution to the good of the whole.

When all is said and done, isn't a champion one who strives for his/her personal best with no regard for what the world sees and rewards? Shouldn't personal best be about what God can depend on you for? Who couldn't cheerfully do a job that pays well? Only a champion can do a job well for the sake of doing it well. How sad that in a world gone mad focusing only on what is due us, we have abandoned the only thing that gives us true purpose and satisfaction. Jim seemed to understand this but probably never knew he was a champion among us. And the world never knew it either. Unfortunately, the world doesn't realize we could use more real champions like him. The people who are supposed to know about these things believe gold medals make for good commercials, after all, aren't you convinced to buy things because a Gold Medalist recommends it?

You know, call me crazy but, frankly, I'd rather trust the unpaid opinion of a hard working, cheerful janitor who has nothing to gain but self-respect.

Whatever you do, work at it with all your heart, as working for the Lord, not for men.

—Colossians 3:23

Fashion Sense

I'm pretty sure I hate to shop for clothing. I much prefer to be doing something else, like, for example, buying groceries, and then stumble across something good, toss it into my cart and hang it in my closet until I need it. Stores that offer groceries and clothing are my best friends. I am only mentioning this, up front, because I have recently had a rather traumatic clothes shopping experience to rant about and I want to establish that I am not a fashion queen. This does not mean, however, that I don't have fashion sense.

Ron and I have a rather limited social life, mostly revolving around family that cares not one twit about how we dress, so, faced with a pending semi-dressy social engagement, I was forced to go seek out and purchase an appropriate outfit. Everything in my closet is more geared to sitting on the screen porch watching the grandkids chase fireflies.

My parameters for the outfit I had in mind were highly defined, but not unreasonable, I thought. I needed something that was black, at least from the waist down, dressy-casual, a sort of jacketed thing that was not quite a suit, maybe with some discrete sparkle (optional), good-fitting (meaning well-built to hide figure flaws). And reasonably priced if not outright cheap.

I started my quest at Lord & Taylors. I have found, in the past, they have GREAT sale racks at the end of the season. On the ride down the elevator to the Big Girl Clothing Department (euphemistically called Women's) I could see huge rounders, literally bulging with great buys. Seventy-five percent off! I admit I was momentarily blinded by the potential of enormous savings but it didn't take long to see there was a profoundly disappointing reason behind the shear number of things available for the low low prices.

This brings me to the heart of my rant.

First of all, I had worked up a sweat, tugging and pulling at the clothes stuffed so tightly together so I quickly skipped over anything that was wool or suede or long-sleeved or turtle-necked. I could hardly breath much less could I desire to try on anything that even remotely resembled cold-weather attire. Where were the end-of-season clothes? In warm climates like Atlanta, in-between clothing is far more useful than season specific garments. There is a genuine dearth of transitional clothing available. This is just an aside and word to the wise for any textile marketer who might happen across this.

But I digress.

The real reason there were so many clothes on those racks was because they were awful! They didn't sell because who would want them? Someone designed these things. Someone must have thought they were just what mature women wanted to wear so they put them through the lengthy process of having them made and brought to market. What a complete waste of energy and materials. Bad choices of fabrics, unfortunate selections of patterns and colors, not to mention abysmal styling. Narrow options ranging from a tiny blue/pink floral print my grandmother might have liked to a sad rip-off version of something my granddaughter might wear. Bows? Croppy little jackets? Flower Power prints reminiscent of the sixties? Are they nuts?

Here's what I think.

The good clothing designers, those who understand the mature woman's preferences, life-styles and physique, are gone. The ones remaining are too young to understand anything about sagging butts, puffy arms and fluffy waistlines. They have no idea what raw silk is or the merits and mystical qualities of gabardine and linen. Apparently, mastering classic line, timeless style and flattering color are the techniques and tools of clothing design artists of the past, who, as I mentioned before, are all retired now.

I did finally find a nice two-piece outfit. Black pant, loosely fitted but not croppy jacket with three quarter length sleeves. Lightweight enough for October in Atlanta, yet dark enough to acknowledge there's been a seasonal change on the calendar. A scattering of gold thread subtly woven in the jacket-top, plus, being on sale for $40, made it fit my criteria as close as was possible. It was a hard won victory, however, because it took exhaustive searching through five stores to accomplish. I felt like a princess who had to kiss a lot of toads to get to her prince. To me, this is consummate waste. Literally thousands upon thousands of unwearable garments hang limply on rack after rack in store after store and who is to blame? Who do we track back to for these crimes against fashion? The fabric mills? The clothing designers? The store buyers? Maybe it is we, the buyers, who are to blame. They give us what we have been willing to settle for. Maybe all those clothes left unsold are clues the fashion market should be considering.

Maybe we should put on our brown and pink Flower Power, croppy jackets, tie the front bows and do a sit in. Puleeeeese!

I cannot and will not cut my conscience to fit this year's fashion.

—Lillian Hellman

Abortion

Abortion is one of those sticky topics I have set aside for a long time, unable to verbally address exactly why I believe it is wrong. One argument, that I hear time and again, is that it isn't specifically addressed in the Bible so why is it an issue with Christians? I think I am ready to answer this, at least to my own satisfaction. Please join me, as I try to figure this out.

In my passionate youth, I was Pro-choice, not because I thought abortion was okay, but because I believed that laws would not stop abortion and would simply create law-breakers out of women and cause them to find unsavory chop-shops to do the job. I reasoned that whatever their rationale for choosing abortion, be it health, financial or emotional, women should be able to make the choice and then deal with eventual personal judgment just as any sinner would. I considered that if a woman wanted an abortion but didn't have one only because of a law, then in her heart, she still had sinned because she desired to step outside of God's perfect will. Even so, then, as now, I did not feel it was my place to judge anyone in this regard. It was basically none of my business what another chose to do. At that point I could not have given a Biblical reason for believing abortion was a sin against moral law.

As I matured in the spirit and I became acquainted with several women who had had abortions in their teens, and dealt with life-long indefinable grief, I began to see another side to the issue; the spiritual side.

I believe humans, created in God's image, body/soul/spirit, each with a life timeline assigned, each with purpose, have a reason to be born. There is no way for me, or anyone else, to know what these reasons are, but nevertheless, I think there is a bigger picture, one which we are too myopic to see. To say there is no great plan simply because we do not see it, is childish at best. Within minutes of conception a human fetus is, by nature, imbued with everything it needs to be human. Is a fetus viable? No. Was Christopher Reeve viable after his accident? No. So is viability the only thing that determines the value of human life, at any stage of development? Are we not continuing to develop even to our last breath?

What about potential? What about spirit and soul? What if every fetus, regardless of imperfection, deformity or intelligence has a purpose that furthers God's will here on earth? Christ said, (Matthew 10:29-31) Are not two sparrows sold for a farthing? And one of them shall not fall on the ground without your Father. But the very hairs on your head are all numbered. Fear ye not therefore, ye are of more value than many sparrows.

A fetus can have hair at the thirteenth week of development. It can't yet live outside the womb, but God knows how many hairs it has. God also knows why it is forming.

In the worship of our advanced intelligence, we often disregard the spirit side of our three-prong existence. We seek only the intelligent ways to define our lives. We look to modern experimentation to make our lives better, healthier, more perfect. Unfortunately, all too often, in the process we lose true perfection. We drift farther and farther away from faith and soul-feeding connection to the Creator who, in His mysterious ways has a plan for us. A plan that often means trial by fire and tribulation. A plan that often includes unexpected, and untimely birth. It also includes miscarriage and naturally aborted humans. Regardless of our lack of understanding, these have purpose too.

We manipulate conception in the name of advanced science and for His reasons, God allows it. Men donate, anonymously, their sperm to sperm banks and father hundreds of children, increasing the odds that these offspring might one day meet, fall in love and marry each other, thus diluting the gene pool. We develop drugs and techniques that seem to prolong life under the guise of making life better, but does it? Is life really improved for all our medical meddling?

Life is a gift from the Creator and we, in our arrogance, think we can outsmart God by giving and taking life ourselves. But we are as foolish as the residents and tower builders of Babel. If we could but humble ourselves and seek to live by faith, not sight, we would find the originally intended balance in the body, the spirit, and the soul. There can be no balance as long as we choose to override God and set our jaws determined to be the masters of our own fate. It is a fool's quest.

There are many things that offend the nature of God that are not specifically outlined for us in the Bible. But they don't have to be. The Bible is not the last spoken word of God. It is only a beginning, a starting place for seeking spiritual growth and a defined path. How can I know this? This knowledge doesn't come from doctrine or religion, it comes from spirit.

I ask Christ for guidance every day. Every day He opens the way for me. More often than not, I begin by reading Scripture to find my answers. Does it say in the Scripture what I should do today? If I wondered about abortion and went to the Bible to find an answer, would I?

Yes, in fact, I would.

Trust in the Lord with all your heart and lean not on your own understanding; In all your ways acknowledge Him and He will make your paths straight.

—Proverbs 3:5-6

On the Water

*R*egardless of how stressed I might be, I find I cannot cling to angst when I'm out on the water. Ron and I took the annual spring trial run on the boat recently and running at full throttle, my hair flapping around like laundry hung out on a windy day, eyes closed, face full tilt to the sun, I could feel my troubles leaving like a fever breaking. I get all inspired when I'm out on the deep water. Within minutes of losing sight of the dock, urges to write rise up as if from hibernation. It occurs to me I think I would write more if I lived on a houseboat. In fact, I don't think I could stop myself.

I see humanity divided into two main groups, and then, of course, into many sub groups, but basically people are either water people or they are land people. And, furthermore, I have found that most water people have deep yearnings to be on or near salt water. If this isn't possible, due to life circumstances, then these water people will always be found on a lake or river, sometimes even a pond has to do. We'd be in a marina somewhere on the Gulf if Ron had his way. No doubt I'd be right there with him, except I have even stronger yearnings to be where family is. I appease him with, "maybe someday." In the meantime, we are content to pack a lunch, speed out to some cove, drop anchor and just be on the water. I can't really explain it, but I do know the experience is not just satisfying, it is the only way I can truly let go. Maybe the rush of the wind and the negative ions from the moist air, not to mention the occasional pungent fishy smell works like aroma therapy. Whatever, it sure cleans out the corners. For a good twenty-four hours after being out on the water, I think more clearly. I swear it.

Out there bobbing around, the boat making lazy circles around the tether of the anchor, is where I have had some of my best, most startlingly dynamic ideas. On this particular trip, however, I just did a little spring cleaning. No good ideas, no story lines or puppet shows. Just finding my balance again. Sorting and filing, I stumbled across a stray thought about last year at this time and how my focus was on Y2K and the uncertainty of the near future. Last May I was busy making plans to spend as much time with the grandkids as possible in the summer months, unsure what kind of summer loomed ahead in the year 2000. It occurred to me that this year is different only because things are still working. There is no defined hard deadline for catastrophe now. This then, seems a bit more dangerous, somehow.

This unsettling thought lead to a recognition that I am not the same person this year that I was this time last year, so this sort of notion doesn't affect me like it would have. While only a year older, chronologically speaking, I am eons older in terms of spirituality. And maybe at least decades older in terms of collected wisdom. I definitely can attribute this to the learning curve I resided in last year. But if I had to choose the most significant thing I absorbed last year, besides how to get on my knees more, I wouldn't know where to begin. If I made a list, learning to can would be at the top and then how to store food and water. But these are only mechanics. Next, I could add that I learned how to interpret double-speak from the economy-driven mass media. And though this was an important lesson to tuck into long term memory if one wishes to be "aware" it doesn't really change anything, other than make one more paranoid and mistrustful.

No, push come to shove, if I had to name the most significant change in me over the course of the past twelve months, I guess I'd have to say it was the loss of future. Simply put, I don't live in the future anymore. Frankly, I can't visualize *someday* anymore. I try to enjoy the roses today, while they are blooming. I appreciate hot showers and electric lights but mostly I touch and feel and breathe deeper today. I know this is a hold-over from the way I felt last year, but if we can't possibly know what tomorrow will bring, why should we waste a precious moment of this day?

We get these things in touchy-feely emails and say, ah, yes, this is so true. But last year I was forced to face that this lesson is not only true, it is the basis for honest living. And one of the most serious decisions I made last year, after I justified spending money on car loads of beans and rice, was that honest living is really where I want to be.

This is the day the Lord hath made, let us rejoice and be glad in it.

Real

I've been holding back, hoping someone would step up and speak out about this worrisome issue, but apparently it falls on me to say the hard words. Getting right to it: wrinkles are not the worst thing that could happen to us.

I know who is behind wrinkle phobia and frankly I'm disappointed but not surprised. The same demographic that coined the phrase, "trust no one over thirty" in the mid-sixties, is now insisting that we all get nipped and tucked so no one will know we are over fifty. How sad are Boomers who can't let go of youth worship? More to the point, whom are we kidding? What are we afraid of? What is so distasteful about the body aging naturally?

Granted, when I look in the mirror in the mornings I see a stranger. The sensation of still feeling young but looking old is not unlike being held prisoner against one's will. But is this a good rationale for having our sagging jowls stretched tightly up behind our ears so that we look like mummies? Does this justify filling our time-lined brows with deadly toxins or puffing out our puckering lips with artificial agents? Does painful surgery make more sense than growing old with grace?

I don't get it but I think it all took a nasty turn along the way when commerce, seeking to pander to aging Boomers, the largest single group of buying public in history, started advertising creams for our hemorrhoids and pills for our acid reflux. Obviously someone noticed we were getting on in years and then some Boomer, recalling the mantra, must have yelled, "not yet!" Now, sprinkled in amongst the ads for financial retirement security and arthritis meds, we get subtle reminders that we ought to hold back the ravages of time with expensive secret formulas. Do you not find it ironic that there is more than one "reality" show devoted to makeovers? This is real?

I don't think so.

Real is the gorgeous platinum of my eighty-year-old mother-in-law's hair. Real is the deep folds in the cheeks of my hard-working father-in-law. Real is the age spots on the back of my dear sister's hands. Real is the thinning hair on my beloved husband's head and the spider-veins behind my knees. This is real life and more important than appearing to be younger than one's age those who know what is real also know what is most important about getting older.

Nearly every collection of quotable quotes includes wise words from Eleanor Roosevelt, such as: "You gain strength, courage, and confidence by every experience in which you really stop to look fear in the face." and: "He who loses money, loses much; He who loses a friend, loses much more; He who loses faith, loses all." Yes, Eleanor gave us many good words to live by and her works and ideals have remained with us long after her life was completed in 1962. It's interesting to note that Eleanor is remembered for her beautiful mind and good heart, not her good looks. She also said, "No one can make you feel inferior without your permission." Personally, I'd choose being remembered for who and what I was inside and what I contributed to the greater good over how young I looked in my coffin.

This is real.

Let us take things as we find them: let us not attempt to distort them into what they are not.... We cannot make facts. All our wishing cannot change them. We must use them.

—John Henry Cardinal Newman

Tadpoles

It went so fast. Hayes, Olivia and I were so busy having fun, we didn't notice that summer was coming to an end. We had planned to have a little ceremony to let our tadpoles go and we didn't get around to it before the school bells started ringing again. So, here I am, all by myself, down at the dock, trying to coax the little black critters out of their safe container – the one we carefully landscaped with rocks and mud and slime from the shallows – so they wouldn't notice they were trapped and being watched. But they don't want to go. We did too good a job making them feel at home, I guess. I have dipped the container on its side and let the lake water rush in and mingle with the old water, trying to fool them. But the tadpoles have dug in to the bottom muck, totally resistant to the whole idea of swimming out into the unknown. I don't really blame them they can't see, like I, the fishes swimming by eager for a tadpole dinner. But, I have a little time, I won't rush them.

While I wait, I'm looking around and feeling not a little sad. The canoe is resting upside down on the dock. The paddle boat is lonely looking, patiently waiting for another adventure. It is still hot like summer but I know this summer is really just a memory now, albeit a collage of very good memories. We did so much this year – starting off with a June trip to the Fernbank Museum to the African exhibit which inspired our creative juices. We found a book on African culture and over the course of June and July built our own replica of a Kenyan village. Then, of course, we pretended to be explorers as we canoed in and out of the roots of mangroves in the coastal waters of West Africa (next cove) to find a place to eat our peanut butter sandwiches. We went swimming in the piranha infested waters (off the dock) and we sat in our hut (the screen porch) under the lazy fan and read our book on Africa and our favorite book, *Where the Sidewalk Ends* by Shel Silverstein, sipping lemonade.

But the most fun we had was reading about tadpoles in the *Pond Book* by Karen Dawes that came with our tadpole tank and then, to our delight, actually finding them in the muddy edges of the lake. On our very first foraging trip we spotted a whole colony of little black wigglers. Of course we recognized them right away because we had pictures. Leaving our footprints in the sludge, we came away with five healthy specimens.

What do you feed tadpoles? We looked it up in the book. Then, everyday, we checked on them, anxiously awaiting signs of change. The Pond Book told us tadpoles turn into frogs in 2 to 16 weeks, depending on the type. Our collection must have been the long cooking kind, because we watched them faithfully for about a month and they had only begun to show signs of changing. Oh well, it didn't really matter – we found lots of other summer things to do, swimming at Bogen Park (oh, that slide!) and movies and nature walks and lots of ice cream eating. Mostly we just celebrated being together - two kids and a Meema.

I need to go cook dinner now, so I turn the tadpole tank up side down slowly. It is time, they have to go on with their lives, to grow up and be frogs. I won't forget this summer though. And I won't forget them, they weren't just ordinary tadpoles. These were our tadpoles. Next year when we hear the froggy chorus heralding in spring I bet Hayes, Olivia and I will be able to tell the new voices, the ones we named Sam, Suzy, Long Tail, Lily Pad and…Prince.

Hey, you just never know.

The tree which moves some to tears of joy is in the eyes of others only a green thing that stands in the way. Some see nature all ridicule and deformity … and some scarce see nature at all. But to the eyes of the man of imagination, nature is imagination itself.

-William Blake

Black Truth

Truth is like silly putty. You can bend it, stretch it, pull it until it is completely unrecognizable from its original form. Regardless, it always returns to the only thing it is whether you want it to or not. - unknown

If you have never had the experience of sitting in a courtroom, listening to someone bear earnest, slanderous false witness against you or someone you love, you will never fully appreciate the importance of the analogy between truth and silly putty.

Since we have a legal system, rather than a justice system, you have no recourse but to take it gracefully on the chin while your character is used for a dartboard. It is in that moment that you hope another old axiom is true, which is, time heals all wounds and wounds all heels. For some, this is little or no comfort. Most people want justice dealt out instantly. We are deluded to expect that unfairness, in any form, should be met with rapid retaliation. This is only because humiliation, outrage, and incense boil up into your chest like heartburn. Naturally you want relief and your first impulse is to believe that somehow setting about to prove what is untrue will reap relief.

We are so temporal, we think we require instant gratification, believing time is our foe instead of our friend. We shake our fists at the injustices we see. Innocents die and murderers walk free. Hateful gossip ruins reputations and causes life altering grief. Thoughtless and/or calculatedly malicious actions foster countless number of senseless troubles. And as bad as these are, none are as insidious as black truth. Unlike a white lie, where the author knows it is untrue, a black truth becomes real to the person who has crafted it. It is a created reality for this person so it becomes real enough for others to be convinced as well. Whole belief systems are often founded on nothing more than a single individual's black truth.

The bad news is, most of us will come up against black truth sooner or later. The good news is, there is a strategy to triumph over it, if you are willing to be patient. We are told we have free will but this only means we are given the opportunity to choose to be vessels of honor or vessels of dishonor. God will use us either way, but if you believe that all things work together for God's good purpose, then you must also believe that He is working good things through you at all times, regardless of how it looks to you. This doesn't mean that you can't stand up for yourself or that you must accept abuse. It only means that you should have developed the fine-tuned listening skills it takes to hear when God is whispering for you to be still and watch. More often than not, through life crisis, He is teaching and it is in these times it behooves us to be fully engaged in a learning mode.

Learning to wait is undoubtedly the hardest lesson in life because we permit the unknown to threaten and overwhelm us. Instead of saying "peace be still", fully trusting the storm to turn, we succumb to the fear of that which seems to be out of our control. We then become victims. If one can find comfort in knowing there is, indeed, a final judgment, one never has to be devastated by black truth. Even if it seems for a time that the whole world is willing to believe the worst of you, you can still choose to be a vessel of honor. Having made that choice, you can be at peace with losing any battle, knowing the war has already been won.

You see, God knows the difference between lies, white lies, black truth and real truth. Not even black truth, though it gathers up followers and devoted believers like a vacuum, can survive the ultimate cleansing power of that which is genuinely true. God sorts it all out in His good time. The irony is, since liars live as though there is no God or final judgment, they won't know how wrong they have been, until it is too late.

If you stand straight, do not fear a crooked shadow.
—Chinese proverb

Ping!

Ping... ping... ping...

*P*ing! Ah, finally. Whew! My first efforts at canning are sealed. Relaxed now, since the pressure canner did not, in fact, blow up – though I was prepared to evacuate for the long ninety minutes– every muscle ridged, ready to respond to the command to flee. But, thank God no need. I step back and admire my first four quarts of canned hamburger, an unfamiliar meaty aroma still hovering in the house; perhaps more accurately described as *clinging*. Yick! Proud as I am, of my efforts, the truth is, the results look disgusting. Never mind, in the dead of winter – the bony knuckles of hunger knocking at my door, I'll see these jars not as science experiments gone awry but as life giving sustenance. And anyway, tomato sauce used liberally can make anything look better. Now, backing off from the smaller view of four, still bubbling jars of gray mystery meat and seeing the larger view of the kitchen where these miracles were prepared.

Oh my.

In the throws of the process I have used every possible surface, three large pots, two small pots, four dishtowels, three large wooden spoons, one Pyrex dish, two canning books, the pressure canner and perhaps five gallons of water. It gives one pause. It makes one wonder, how important, in the scheme of things, is hamburger, after all. As I begin the task of cleaning up I mull this over and before the last pot is washed, dried and stored away I come to this conclusion: what is important about canned hamburger is that I have learned how to do it. In this Information Age we have become so dependent on artificial intelligence, we have let go of and forgotten the most basic skills of survival. We lean on and trust our welfare and well-being to devices of questionable reliability in the ambiguous name of progress and advanced civilization. In the past half year, spent in a vigorous learning curve, desperately regaining a mere portion of the skills my mother took for granted, I have also rediscovered what is more important than vast amounts of superfluous data. I have been reacquainted with the instruction and testing of my willingness to learn how to learn to be self-sufficient. Interestingly enough, this, in turn, has drawn me closer to God. For is it not our willingness to accept the responsibility for ourselves that reveals to us our responsibility to God and what He expects of us? We do, after all, have a commission to seek to be worthy. It is the least we can do with what God has blessed us with. One thing is for sure – it makes no sense to be helpless. How much wiser it is to be prepared for contingency; how much more valuable is self-reliance over dependency? Four quarts of hamburger waiting in my pantry isn't much, I can eat them, regardless of what happens. But learning how to can has reacquainted me with my willingness to be held accountable for what happens to me. Both humility and self-esteem experienced simultaneously.

Amazing.

I have found in life that if you want a miracle you first need to do whatever it is you can do – if that's to plant, then plant; if it is to read, then read; if it is to change, then change; if it is to study, then study; if it is to work, then work; whatever you have to do. And then you will be well on your way of doing the labor that works miracles.

–Jim Rohn

Success

*T*here is a point, somewhere just after I begin a creative endeavor where I ask myself whatever gave me the idea I could accomplish such a thing. Doesn't matter what it is, writing, painting, sewing, or puppet show production. Nor does it matter how many times I have done something similar, I begin anew each time. And each time I wonder if this will be the attempt that does me in, believing this is *when* not *if*. I used to think I was grossly deficient in the self-confidence department, now I have come to recognize this head game as an intrigal part of my creative process. Seems, and I'm only guessing here, I allow the ever cynical left side of my brain to taunt and tease the tender, more vulnerable right side as a check and balance system. Simply put, it keeps me humble. It also insures I never reach a place where I consider myself to be at a pinnacle of achievement. It would be the greatest embarrassment of my life to think I had finally done something to crow about only to discover I was really something less than mediocre all along. I've seen others fall into this pit and I'm sure I don't want to go there. If I am mediocre, I want to know it from the outset. I can handle mediocrity if I know in my heart I gave it my best shot and still came up wanting. After all, this is entirely different from being mediocre for laziness or quitting in midstream, defeated by the difficulty of the enterprise.

So, with no illusions about my potential or raw skills, fully aware I am awash with both, what I am is nothing more than a work in progress, never fully complete. This is, in many ways, better than having arrived anyway. So long as I am honest with myself where I am in the journey I can maintain the enthusiasm necessary to carry forward even when understanding there isn't a defined destination. Though, in some areas, I have at last hit a wall and I accept that future improvements will be minimal at best. With this I have made my peace. But so long as I remain open to suggestions and ever mindful that improvements, however small are possible, I keep moving. The trick is to recognize and seize on opportunities to expand and to be always at the ready to dive in fearlessly.

Disregarding all axioms on how to be successful, I engage in first gear fully expecting to fail. But hear me out because I have stumbled across a secret revealing what defines true success, which is nothing more than the simple act of trying and then trying again. Success is just a process. There is a famous quote attributed to Robert Fulghum, "If at first you don't succeed, redefine success." So I submit a new axiom - *I try, therefore I succeed*.

Once you grasp the simplicity of this concept, you understand that regardless of how society interprets success, those of us who persevere inspite of never finding fame or fortune, are those who live successfully. Not because we reach a specified goal, but because, neither obscurity nor lack of riches can limit someone who is sincerely committed to continued personal growth.

If persistence promotes continued growth and success is defined by persistence, then I'm proud to say I'm right on track.

Success is going from failure to failure without loss of enthusiasm.

-Winston Churchill

Snow Day

A snow day is a gift. Ask any kid who doesn't have to go to school because of snow. There certainly is nothing that arouses the kid in me like awakening to find the world outside my window has been transformed into a Christmas card. Here on the lake, the experience is doubley exhilarating. Growing up in Houston, I missed out on snow days. As quickly as I can, I dig out my boots, hat and warm gloves, grab my camera and trek off on a quest to find remnants of the dreams of my childhood.

For less than an hour I am an explorer of a new world.

Before I choose my path, I stop to listen to the garden. It is painfully quiet. The birds are too busy trying to stay warm to sing. The azaleas are sleeping, all tucked in. The arbor swing sits motionless, outlined with a thick highlight of white. The Japanese Maple looks like a wire sculpture.

I strain to hear beyond the silence. But all sound is muffled today. I move on with anticipation. I discover the path to the lake is hidden but it doesn't matter because my feet remember.

I expect to find deer tracks. We had watched a six-point buck and two does on Christmas morning. But surprisingly my footprints are the first to break the pristine surface. Once I have made it to the beach, I know I have to tread carefully, though. Five inches of snow can easily hide the treacherous landscape of the slope. Carved up by erosion and the relentless decline of the lake level, one could easily step into a hole or crevice. I make a mental note to retrace my footprints back. At least they are proven steps thus far.

I had planned to go onto the dock and take a picture from the upper deck. But the ramp was so steep I had a disturbing image of me sliding down and off into the chilly water. The vision made me shiver. No. I'm an explorer today, not a fool. Recalling the adage about descretion and valor, I decide instead to hike to the edge of the lake. I pause to look at our neighbor's sail boat. It's in peaceful repose now like the azaleas. Briefly,

I tap into a sweet dream of summer, balmy breeze pushing at the sheets, full out. Seems far away today. Far, far away.

When I make it to the water's edge I am amazed at how the shore line looks with the water level so low. This span of beach isn't even here when the lake is at full pool. Will this be the new shoreline? Will Spring bring the rain we need? Only God knows.

Again I strain to study the silence. And then I realize, there is no such thing as silence. Not here in the great outdoors, anyway. You just have to retrain your civilized ear to tune in the subtle whispers. There is the sound of wind in the tops of the old pines across the lake. There is a tinkling from someone's wind chime. There is water lapping at the sides of the docks. Cold, cold water sounds.

When finally I am ready to head back I find I've stepped into a sudden blizzard. A mini blizzard. I can't tell if it is coming from the sky or just the trees shaking themselves. Maybe both. In a matter of seconds I am coated like the landscape and my camera is wet. I catch myself smiling. I wonder if I made a snow angel, would I be able to get up. Probably not easily, anyway, is my conclusion. I press onward.

Down the path, I notice a pair of old logs. They look so cold. Staring at them makes me suddenly grateful for the pot of chili simmering on the stove and the promise of a steaming cup of coffee waiting for me.

The explorer sets her compass for the warmth of home.

Thank you, Father for this snow day.

In the depths of winter, I finally learned that within me there lay an invincible summer.

-Albert Camus

Volunteering

I'm sitting here at the security desk on the last Friday of the school year 2004 typing on my iBook. It's my job to make sure those who enter this building are not only who they say they are but have good reason to be here. This is a volunteer position and one of several hats I wear as a contributor to the common good of Rock Springs Elementary School. It is also my next to last year to be a member of the huge volunteer force, comprised of parents and grandparents, who give countless hours to the process of assisting the staff to make this school run like a well-greased machine. I fall into the latter group (grandparent) and I graduate next year as my granddaughter moves on to middle school.

I can tell already that it's going to be a bittersweet experience for me to bid farewell next year. I fully expect I'll be weepy for most of the month of May 2005. For one thing, it will mean the obvious that Olivia is growing up and I am growing older. But for another, it might possibly be the end of my elementary school volunteering, one I have cherished off and on since 1972. The aging tired part of me is ready to move on and let the younger mothers take up the task, and the fun loving part of me rails against giving up the pleasure and self-satisfaction.

I started volunteering as a young mother of three before the term *stayathomemom* (yes, that's one word) was coined. Volunteering seemed the best way to channel all of my energy and creativity, finding a better use for my intelligence than watching soaps all day, and still be available to the kids when they were home from school. Between PTA, Camp Fire and Boy Scouts, some years I was spread pretty thin, often attending as many as a dozen meetings a month plus all the time spent planning and executing committee work. I didn't realize it at the time, while I was fully immersed in the daily routine, but all that practice of organizational skills looked great on my resume when it was time for me to step back into the paid work force as my kids moved into their adult lives. This is a side benefit of volunteering that one doesn't consider when signing up to work long hours for free, however.

There are many others, perhaps, if not certainly, more important.

First and foremost, time freely given is rewarded two-fold, by a profound sense of accomplishment and profuse appreciation from those on the receiving end. The single most eye-opening truth I experienced, once I reentered the corporate world, was that whereas your best is always good enough while in a volunteer capacity it isn't always thus in the work place when a paycheck sums up your worth. The person issuing the check may have a completely different perspective on what you should be able to accomplish in a given period of time. Unfortunately, this might not agree with your point of view, limitations or enthusiasm. The subtle dynamic underneath it all is that those who volunteer nearly always do so because they want to, not because they have to which isn't always true with a paying job. The human psyche is complex, thus it often happens that volunteers give better than their best because the drive to feel worthwhile for effort expended is always rewarded with something more esthetic and less definable than cold hard cash. In fact, the value of volunteering cannot effectively be compared to work done for hire. It's bananas and mangos.

The list of places that need and welcome volunteers would fill a large volume and the need grows annually. Every year schools and youth groups scramble to fill positions of leadership with willing manpower. Mores the pity, civic and local organizations that reach out to the ever increasing needs of community find themselves depending on fewer and fewer members. This is a mystery to me, and a crying shame, because I know from first hand experience that volunteering opens doors and provides immeasurable good for not only the organization but also for the one volunteering. It's win/win. The years I clocked in and collected my pay-checks were pretty much their own reward. The years I have spent making things better or easier for those who are making things better for others will continue to reward me for the remainder of my life. If you ever wake up and wonder what to do with spare time, try volunteering.

It will make you rich. I promise.

Playhouse

Got a minute? Dust off your imagination and take a tour with me.

It's summer 1957. Even in the bright daylight it is dark in here but the eyes gradually become accustomed. Hodge podge of unrelated, discarded furniture. Rough wooden boxes occasionally sting and leave slivers in little fingers. A faded yellow rocker, kid-sized, one man's trash, a ten year old's treasure. An old Hollywood sofa bed. Brown and smelly. A lethal combination of dust and dog. The walls are raw but good for writing on. A name, a phone number. A primitive drawing. The ceiling is bare rafters. Great for suspending temporary fabric walls. Also great for harboring wasp colonies.

A six foot ladder. The top becomes an entire second floor of a sprawling mansion. The movie star descends gracefully to the marble foyer and greets her guests. She laughs lightly and charms her way around the gracious ballroom astounding everyone with her wit and cleverness. The phone rings. She accepts devastating news. She excuses herself and retires to her quarters. A grand exit up the winding staircase. Everyone would be so shocked and dismayed over her suicide. A nice little dramatic ending but not as compelling as the Princess imprisoned in the highest turret of the Giant's cold, dank castle. Her golden locks float easily around her shoulders like a silken mantle... or a bunch of mom's old nylon stockings. She looks longingly out of the window at the tree tops and the misty countryside. She does so need her Prince to come. She passes the time singing sad songs in the most beautiful voice ever known to man. She waits patiently perched for hours on the spot that reads. WARNING, NOT A STEP.

Arranging, rearranging. Rickety chairs, boxes, little broken tables. Make them fit the daydream. Work around the nasty burlap curtain that conceals the lawn mower but can't hold back the acrid odor of sour grass and gasoline; a concession with The Dad for the shared use of this space.

Play House

Arranging and rearranging. The kitchen is a sagging little shelf suspended limply between two wall studs. Jars of tiny bits and pieces of collected things cling together on one end trying not to slide forward to sudden splintering on the rough concrete floor. An old linoleum surfaced counter top is a workspace for the amazing concoctions of grass and mud pies. A world renown chef humbly accepts the praise for her latest recipe for goulash. The secret ingredient is closely guarded.

Faded crayon marks outline the remains of paths. Trails through Candy Land. The ladder/mountain has whipped cream on its peak. Some wall studs bear red stripes, candy cane sentinels. The Candy Land Fairy Princess emerges from her sugar cottage. Amana refrigerator box. THIS SIDE UP. She sparkles and flutters about tending to all the little creatures of the forest. She is so wise and they love her so. She always has the answers. Except how to open the window. Always stuck. And the other one won't stay open without a stick to prop it. But it only matters in the summer months when the soaring temperature swells up the pine walls and makes the knots weep sticky, amber tears. In the heat, the pine sap and the gasoline fumes mingle and synergize. It smells explosive.

Outside, the concrete step-up runs the length of the front of the playhouse. A hopscotch grid is permanently etched into the surface. A good place to escape the oxygen deficient atmosphere. An old pine tree provides hit and miss shade to this spot in the afternoon. Lindy, the English girl, brings new games and great skill to this place. She also brings wonderful English books. Us Dogs is read uninterruptedly in the yellow upholstered rocker in one sitting. A sad ending. A new and painful experience full of sobbing, salty, last page tears and delicious growth.

An idea! Other books. Gathered from everywhere. Old moldy books, paperbacks and new Readers Digest Condensed books. A library. The librarian is very strict. She is a rock. No noise allowed. No talking, no loud movements. This is a quiet place, a place for reflection and serious study. But an unfortunate incident. Something to do with the entire works of Mark Twain left in the yard. Rain. LIBRARY CLOSED. Books confiscated by The Mom. Back to the lone reader in the yellow upholstered rocker.

Chairs and tables and boxes in neat rows. A Blackboard. Students of all shapes and sizes and species. One is spotted brown and white. She is dressed in a tee shirt and baby bonnet. This is not a happy student. She looks longingly backward towards the door. She has a plan but she is patient. The teacher begins class. She is brilliant. Math, English, History a little Geography. The teacher turns to write large chalky letters on the blackboard. The student sees her opening and escapes out the door barking wildly at some imagined hostile intruder. Recess. Time to swing for a while. Large, wooden swing set in the shadow of the playhouse. Great ideas are sometimes born here where the closest thing to independent flight is often attempted. Pumping and straining every muscle to toe touch the lowest branch on the world's largest pine tree. A tree held together with several pounds of ten penny nails. A little carpentry practice. The Dad always wondering where his nails disappear to. This tree is also keeper of the basketball hoop. No net. Many one- on- one games called HORSE with a brother who always wins. Swinging higher and higher. This time, so high the chain relaxes at the top of the arc and there is a millisecond where gravity is defied. A bargain struck with God to allow one hour of unrestrained flight through the clouds. No one would ever find out. A bargain is a bargain. Especially with God.

Recess over. Back to work. Star student hiding. Never mind. Arranging and rearranging. A boat. A hospital. A cave. A bank. Never-Never land. A home, but only in the daylight. No electricity. Too many dangerous fumes for candlelight.

Dusk ends much more than just the day. There's tomorrow. Another day will shed its light on this magic place that inspires exploration, expansion and rehearsal for all the possibilities. It is a parallel universe without limits or boundaries; no dimensions of height, width, or length. To open the wooden door and cross the threshold is not to enter this physical space, but rather to penetrate the heart and soul of a dreamer.

Play is the exultation of the possible.
—Martin Buber

Safe

Sometimes you're just chugging along and suddenly life jumps up and spikes you to the ground like a volleyball. You can't believe it. You don't even know how to react because you are in shock from the jolt. It could be anything, financial setback, sudden illness, a family death or upheaval. One day you're all cozy in status quo and the next you're struggling to survive or regain your equilibrium.

Trouble is something we can never be completely prepared for or shielded from either, no matter how hard we try to buffer ourselves. However we cannot live in constant expectation of worse case scenario because living in daily fear of trouble is not living at all, rather it's standing guard while life marches past, conversely, we cannot ignore that trouble can happen at anytime and usually without warning.

Life can never be fully trouble proof nor safe either but "trouble-free and safe" has become a mantra whispered in our ears and taught to us as though it were a natural right. In fact, we seem to have become fixated with all things safe.

I watch with amazement as this new standard has slowly evolved. I don't know how it began but it seems that in all ways, in all things, we have been brainwashed to believe that our lives can and should be without trouble and completely safe if we are simply vigilant enough. We can avoid the flu if we take shots, we can protect ourselves from all manner of larceny, theft, fire, accidents (pick one) if we use caution and load up with insurance. We can count on government and consumer advocates to monitor any and all things potentially harmful to us. If we read warning labels and cautionary statements we can reduce the chance of electric shock, skin broken or blood spilled. And even when we disregard the warnings, we can always blame manufacturers if we misuse a product that injures us.

Apparently pain and suffering has a hefty dollar value now.

Unfortunately, regardless what we have been told, living in this world remains naturally full of risk. Here's a newsflash: safe is not a right bestowed on us at birth. We come into this world without guarantees. The human infant is hardwired to accept risk as a given or no one would ever learn to walk upright. New dangers emerge daily; we cannot stop them nor avoid them.

And if we could, should we?

Progress is the end product of trial and error. Innovation is the result of risk takers stepping outside of what is sure. Pioneers who strike out for new territory often die trying. Trouble and tribulation are the knives that carve character into life. Though there is nothing inherently wrong with being safe, it's only a small part of what is worthwhile about living. Sometimes standing up to conflict and surviving is ten times more satisfying than hiding behind security. To spend our days obsessed with avoiding every possible scenario of strife is to deny us opportunities for growth. Yes, risk is dangerous and sometimes we get hurt, even irreparably. Sometimes the price seems too high. But wisdom is rarely born of status quo and what is wisdom worth? How valuable is courage that stares squarely in the face of insurmountable odds and emerges triumphant?

If I had to choose, I'd pick courage that overcomes rather than security that shields because the myth of life that is trouble free and safe was created to sell product and service not preserve us from harm. Safe and secure does not always guarantee quality of life either anymore than wealth insures happiness.

Here's an irony: a society obsessed with being safe at all times is already enslaved to fear. Fear is the enemy of successful living because it is like a drug that disables the problem solving function in the brain.

When we are too afraid to risk reaching for our own solutions our focus is blurred and we never see it coming when the hammer of enslavement falls.

Those who would give up essential liberty to purchase a little temporary safety, deserve neither liberty nor safety.

— Benjamin Franklin

Sunset Point

*B*ehind the lake house where we used to live, there's an old stadium seat on the point of the peninsula. The realtor who sold us the house referred to it as a "million dollar view". The seat was put there, I assume, eons ago, by someone who wanted to sit and watch the sunsets and the sailboats from Lanier Sailing Club. From our house it was a small hike and then a short climb to get up to the grassy bluff where the seat was positioned for the best viewing. The effort is worth it, though, because from that advantage there was an incredible panorama of the water and sometimes I was held there, spellbound. On a clear day you could see Sawnee Mountain and Booger Hill in Cumming. This is where I went when I needed to think.

There are so many benefits to living on the lake, I can't begin to list them. There are disadvantages as well, but most of those involve the carelessness of visitors and shortsided decisions made by people in power to determine the future of the lake. Recently, one Saturday morning, when our radio alarm tuned into O'Neill Williams, Great Outdoors Show, half asleep I heard a caller ask O'Neill what could be done about the pollution in Lake Allatoona that is ruining it. Fishermen now refer to this once beautiful body of water as The Dead Sea. O'Neill admitted he didn't know what could be done and offered it was a political problem with development by big business and land gobblers at the root of most of the dilemma. It was his opinion that nothing could happen to reverse the damage done that is killing the wildlife and ultimately the lake because when there is big money to be made, nothing else matters - not even the future of Cobb county's drinking water.

Suddenly, I was wide awake. I started thinking. Big Business. Big Money. Big Housing Developments. Decision makers siding with money over prudence. Small municipalities and county officials zoning with only income in mind, then petitioning to be allowed to dump millions of gallons of treated sewage into the lake, even when the EPA has warned against it. Big Landfills that will eventually leach toxic chemicals into the water. Lake Lanier. Destined to be another Dead Sea?

I was haunted by this for days. I'm not an alarmist. I'm not a pessimist. But I do love this lake and Ron and I do our small part to take care of it even if all that means is keeping the beach around our dock cleared of Styrofoam and other trash that floats up. Some of this is swept off other docks in storms, some of it is caused by thoughtless people dumping out of their boats. These people, who only come on the weekends to enjoy the pleasures of this exquisite place don't live here, so they don't care where their trash ends up. Even so, all the trash in the lake left behind by fun-seekers do not contribute near the pollution that weed-killers and fertilizers do. Then burden the perimeter of the lake with septic tanks that often seep and houseboaters who ignore the no-waste dumping laws and last but not least mix in manufacturing, processing and industrial waste and you have a deadly formula. If natural erosion was not enough, even the silt that slides in from and during housing development is slowly choking the lake.

I think about this now because I am a grandmother and wonder what will be left of this lake, if these damaging factors are left unchecked, when my grandchildren are raising their families. When officials are willing to sacrifice the future for present profit, I wonder what can they be thinking?

We believe we are in control of our lives but we are so busy living our lives we entrust the business of our precious future to others; others who often are only thinking about myopic short term gains. This, then, leaves us at their mercy.

From Sunset Point, every clear evening, I could watch a heavy orange sun stain a glimmering corridor on the vast water that made up our back yard. It's hard to imagine not being able to hear the loons calling or see the gulls in a feeding frenzy where the shad are chased to the surface by the big game fish. I have never been able to take these everyday wonders for granted and now I commit them to memory and then to paper because it might be all I have left to bequeath our children and theirs.

For what good can riches do, or might, or fame or power, if ne're again there blooms the sweet and fragrant flower...

Warm

I'm sitting in my snug heated office, sipping on hot cocoa while I type this. It's not so cold for January, here in North Georgia, but it's definitely cold enough to keep me inside where it is warm.

I think I should feel somewhat guilty that I am comfortable because I know there are people, many, many people, less fortunate than I, who are miserable right now. Many of these live in the northeast, holding on, as best they can, against the piercing cold that has gripped that region this winter. For this reason I am writing today because this is on my mind – the bitter, unrelenting cold and what it does to hope – because I know someone who is suffering for it and I am helpless to render not much more than superficial aid to her. She is far away in a small community in Upstate New York and she is freezing.

I also think about the other little families and single individuals who don't have enough heat or garments to protect them from the winter weather. I think about the civic and volunteer organizations that do everything they can but whose funds are already spread too thinly among the growing numbers of the needy. And I think about the callous disregard for the basic requirements of life by a nation of people that is literally overwhelmed with abundance and obscene opulence.

It doesn't seem right. Now don't get me wrong, I'm not a Marxist. I believe that anyone who is willing to work and earn a good living should also reap the rewards of their labor and enjoy it. I'm not wailing the injustices of the poor while shaking my fists at the rich. I believe that where there's a will there is a way and that many unfortunate people could reverse their lot in life with just a small amount of effort. But there are plenty of homeless and downtrodden who simply have lost the will to lift themselves up. They don't have the strength and they've lost heart.

In the thirties, a similar thing occurred, even after and notwithstanding all the government programs put into place to stimulate the economy

I Was Just Thinking

after the Crash, people were so beat down by the daily struggle to survive that they couldn't see anything to hope for. This is what happens when you go to bed cold and hungry. The energy to think ahead evaporates into wisps of vapor along with your body heat.

I heard our President tell us he is planning to throw a trillion dollars at outer space over the next decade. A trillion. There's a number for you. Did you know that if you started as a baby, counting, you still could not count up to a trillion in your lifetime?

If I had a vote, I'd say, let's feed and clothe and house the needy in this country first. Let's make sure human life right now, right here, is worth living. I bet we'd still have a bunch left over to send spacecraft to dead planets in the quest to study where the human race came from.

Not everyone can be rich and Christ told us we would have the poor with us always. But what good is it to find out where we came from if we can't see who we have become?

In the final analysis, the questions of why bad things happen to good people transmutes itself into some very different questions, no longer asking why something happened, but asking how we will respond, what we intend to do now that it happened.

—Harold S. Kushner

Paper

*W*ords would not come. Stunned and muddled, like the rest of the world, for several days following September 11, 2001, I found it difficult to even think in complete sentences. A friend suggested I write. But I could not find the words to write. For a devoted wordsmith, such as I, this was not unlike taping my mouth shut and tying my hands behind my back. Another friend suggested we all back off watching the 24-hour news coverage and try to occupy ourselves with other things so as not to allow the jaws of despair to swallow us up. But I couldn't stop watching; committed to keeping a vigil in case something worse might be about to befall us. And I believe I watched also because it allowed me to help shoulder, at least spiritually, the anguish of those caught in the middle of the nightmare. I could send up specific prayers if I monitored every thing that was happening minute by minute.

By Wednesday, much of the reporting was repetitious, but I watched anyway, hoping perhaps I'd be viewing when a miracle occurred like a living soul removed from the rubble. And then late Thursday evening, by way of filling in the long hours, there was a report of a group of architectural engineers who had begun testing the makeup of the thick powder that once was the World Trade Center. They were not surprised to find it was made of fine particles of glass, concrete, steel, gypsum, marble and granite. Two and one half million tons of strong, rigid material reduced to a fine powder in a matter of minutes.

But that was not the end of the report. What was most phenomenal was that, in spite of the bomb like force that pulverized the dense, solid materials that just hours before had formed two tall buildings, tons of paper floated out and had landed gently on the ground, unburned and intact.

Paper. Fragile, easy to tear, combustible, paper. That spoke to me, and gave me back my words with a whispered message.

I Was Just Thinking

    We need to be like paper. Not steel. Not granite. Not concrete. If we are to survive against the fury of unspeakable evil, we need to be light enough to float. When unexpected forces blow against us, we need to be able to use the blast to propel us instead of being consumed by it. Unfortunately, this means we need to off load some weight. We need to rid ourselves of those especially heavy things like vengeance, selfishness, and hatred. We also need to shed pridefulness, meanness and lack of humility. To put it bluntly, we all just weigh too much and this extra, unnecessary tonnage makes us vulnerable to being crushed. It is when we are weighted down with sin and rebellion that God is more likely to break us.

    This is a subtle lesson, for sure. But it isn't a stretch, by any means. It is no secret that the less we carry around inside, the lighter we are. The lighter we are, the easier it is for God to use us. When He can use us, the closer we are to Him and thus the more He carries for us. The more He carries, the lighter we are.

    Nevertheless, there are those who are simply determined to carry large loads around with them. They see themselves as steel or granite. Invincible. They think they can only depend on their own ability to reason and their own might to defend themselves. It should be noted that today, in New York City, there is a lot of undamaged, simple paper resting lightly on the ruins of descecrated strength.

    Frankly, I'd rather be paper. That way, God can fold me and put me in His pocket.

> *When a man's ways please Jehovah, He maketh even his enemies to be at peace with him.*
>
> —*Proverbs 16:7*

Lids

In January 2005, I realized that I have been writing this column, *I Was Just Thinking,* for fifteen years. It has appeared in the Buford Free Delivery for the last ten but it started out as a monthly addition to The Trails (Norcross) neighborhood newsletter that I put out as part of my duties as the association secretary. One month I had a space to fill so I wrote a little essay, titled it and then I did it again the following month. When it occurred to me that I might turn it into an ongoing column instantly I was awash with self-doubt. How would I ever find enough to write about? How long would it be before I ran out of material?

As a hedge against the dreaded writer's block, I spent a dedicated two weeks and whipped out a year's worth, twelve columns in all. This gave me a nice comfort zone so I'd never have to sweat missing a deadline. I hate missing deadlines. In time, eventually, I grew comfortable enough to use up all my back-log and then depended only on making notes whenever some topic sparked my interest. Sometimes, cleaning out my old computer files, I still run across my notes and wonder what could have possibly been going on in my head at the moment I so cryptically typed them down. Column Ideas – Vanilla, Brass, Junk, Moving, Weeds. Obviously, I should have been more specific.

Even as the years rolled on and I found my groove wherein there was no minutia that escaped my scrutiny and about which I couldn't pound out a minimum of six hundred words, I still harbored a tiny reservation that one day I'd finally reach the edge of the world and draw a big blank. To insure against this I have always kept a reserve idea for a column; my fall-back position. I'm amazed that only once have I had to pull up the reserve and use it. And this was because of a family crisis, not writer's block. So, important to me, psychologically speaking, has been this safety net, that immediately that I had used it, I replaced it with another. Thus far I have not used the replacement. Until today.

I Was Just Thinking

But today, I am not using my back-up column because I am out of ideas, I am using it because I need to air out this annoyance. I need some commisseration, some sympathy. Some suggestions about how to solve this issue. I need help.

This column is about food storage lids. You know what I am talking about.

Today, after lunch, all I wanted to do was put away the soup. Ron watched as I dug fruitlessly in the two drawers where I store those assorted sized plastic bottoms and lids. I'd pull out a bottom that was the correct size and then five lids that didn't fit it. Soon I had the whole counter top covered with bottoms and lids – none of which matched each other.

Ron suggests that bottoms and lids should be tethered together somehow. I'm not so sure this is the answer. I really don't have an answer, just questions. Is this a modern problem? I don't recall my mom having this bottom/lid issue. She recycled mayo jars. Maybe it's just me.

Anyway, I feel better for having brought this out into the open. The soup is still in need of a lid and I'll come up with something. There's always the mayo jar I washed out last week and saved. At least it has its lid. Ironic isn't it?

And then, of course, I'll need to come up with another back-up column topic to replace this one. No problem.

Socks.

I like nonsense, it wakes up the brain cells. Fantasy is a necessary ingredient in living, it's a way of looking at life through the wrong end of a telescope. Which is what I do, and that enables you to laugh at life's realities.

—Dr. Seuss

Last Word

What a journey this has been. Digging out and spending time with my early writings has given me a rare opportunity.

I never equated *I Was Just Thinking* with journaling but, in fact, that is exactly what it has been. Twelve (plus) columns a year for sixteen years added up to just over two hundred. I purposely, and mercifully, left out most of the older pieces because I would have been compelled to edit and improve them, which would have represented me untruthfully. I am not now who I was when I began. I am fuller and wider, both literally and figuratively and the older writings revealed this to me. In a nutshell, I have grown.

And that's the point of journaling, isn't it? It's not only about remembering; it's tracking growth, assessing and taking inventory.

Journaling is like watching an old video of ourselves. Sometimes we are surprised by what we see, sometimes we like it, sometimes we don't but at least we get to face it and take stock so we can figure out where we need to go next.

We do not grow absolutely, chronologically. We grow sometimes in one dimension, and not in another; unevenly. We grow partially. We are relative. We are mature in one realm, childish in another. The past, present, and future mingle and pull us backward, forward, or fix us in the present. We are made up of layers, cells, constellations.

—Anais Nin

April S Fields is a writer/photographer/publisher and keeper of all secrets for six grandchildren. She lives with her husband Ron on Lake Lanier in Northern Georgia.

Her writing credits include, but are not limited to, puppet stories, three fiction short stories published in two O, Georgia! anthologies, two articles (she was actually paid for) in the Photo District News and Low-Carb Energy Magazine, more than two hundred *I Was Just Thinking* columns in several Northeast Georgia publications, and a cookbook, *101 Low-Carb and Sugarfree Dessert Recipes*.

Email her at info@faithfulpublishing.com

When I was four, I would sit for hours with a book in my lap, willing the words to finally speak to me. I don't recall the moment I first began to read. I only know I have never gotten over it.

-April S Fields

Books that inspire from Faithful Publishing

Sovereign God - For Us and Through Us
David Eells - ISBN - 09759941-3-1

Simple Giving Crafts
Vivian Peritts - ISBN - 09759941-1-5

The Tithe That Binds
Rory O Moore - ISBN - 09759941-5-8

Pale As The Moon
Donna Campbell Smith - ISBN - 09759941-6-6

I Was Just Thinking
April S Fields - ISBN - 09759941-8-2

www.faithfulpublishing.com
888-860-5394